eurolingua
English 1A

W0416523

Cornelsen

eurolingua English 1A

Englisch für Erwachsene

Bearbeitung und Redaktion:
Susanne Self

Beratende Mitwirkung:
Dr. Hansjörg Frommer (VHS Karlsruhe), Dr. Hermann Funk (GhK Kassel), Inge-Anna Koleff (VHS Wien), Eva-Maria Meyer-Dammann (VHS Heidelberg), Sabine Rosenfeld (KVHS Saarlouis), Pierre Sommet (VHS Krefeld), Jacqueline Sword (VHS Hannover), Dr. Axel Vielau (VHS Oldenburg), John Waldron (VHS Herrenberg), Dr. Erich Zehnder (Mainz)

Redaktionelle Mitarbeit:
Christine House, Maria Larscheid

Layout und Umschlaggestaltung: Regelindis Westphal
Illustrationen: Laurent Lalo, Robert Broomfield, Carol Daniel

Erläuterung der Symbole

- Der Text ist auf Kassette oder CD zu hören
- schriftliche Übung
- ► ► „Kettenübung"
- ► ◄ „Partnerübung": Sie arbeiten zu zweit
- Sie arbeiten zu dritt
- Sie bilden eine kleine Arbeitsgruppe
- Im Lernerhandbuch finden Sie unter diesem Stichwort weitere Informationen
- Die Lösung der Aufgabe steht im Schlüssel

1. Auflage 1996 Druck 4 3 2 1 Jahr 99 98 97 96

Autor der Originalausgabe: Andrew Littlejohn
Wissenschaftliche Beratung für die Originalausgabe:
Daniel Coste, Anthony Fitzpatrick, Henri Holec, Ernesto Martín Peris, René Richterich, Jan Van Ek

Satz: Satzinform, Berlin

Repro: CRIS, Berlin; Satzinform, Berlin

Druck: Cornelsen Druck, Berlin

Buchbinderei: Fritzsche-Ludwig, Berlin

ISBN 3-464-21016-2
Bestellnummer: 210162

gedruckt auf säurefreiem Papier, umweltschonend hergestellt aus chlorfrei gebleichten Faserstoffen

HINWEISE

Der vorliegende Band 1 A von **eurolingua English** ist der erste Teilband des insgesamt 3-bändigen Englischlehrwerks, mit dem Sie das Niveau des Zertifikats des Deutschen Volkshochschulverbandes erreichen – und die Prüfung bestehen können.

Dieser Band wird Sie während des Kurses und zu Hause beim Englischlernen und Üben begleiten.

Das Kursteilnehmerbuch beinhaltet:

- das Material, das Sie im Kurs benötigen (Texte und Übungen), und die Materialien, die Sie zu Hause zur Nacharbeit noch einmal anschauen und bearbeiten sollten;
- ein kleines Vokabel-Taschenbuch, mit dem Sie auch unterwegs die Vokabeln nachschlagen und lernen können.

Das Kursteilnehmerbuch

Wenn Sie das Buch durchblättern, stellen Sie fest, daß es 12 *Units*, 5 *Options* und einen Anhang enthält.

Die 12 *Units* beinhalten in der Reihenfolge einer sinnvollen Bearbeitung alle Materialien, die zum Lernen benötigt werden: Texte, Übungen, Grammatik, landeskundliche Informationen, Hilfen zur Verbesserung Ihrer Lerntechniken.

Die *Options* enthalten mit unterschiedlicher Gewichtung zusätzliche Texte, erweiternde Grammatik- und Vokabelübungen sowie weitere lerntechnische Hilfen.

Im Anhang finden Sie eine alphabetische Vokabelliste mit den jeweiligen Fundstellen und Übersetzungen, diejenigen Hörtexte, die sich nur auf der Kassette befinden, den Übungsschlüssel sowie eine Liste der englischen Redewendungen, die Sie im Kurs benötigen.

Im Vokabel-Taschenbuch

stehen alle neuen Vokabeln in der Reihenfolge ihres Auftretens, mit Aussprachehilfe, Übersetzung und einem Beispielsatz. Vokabeln, die Sie lernen sollten, sind **fett** gedruckt, solche, die nur verstanden werden müssen, sind ***kursiv*** gedruckt.

Die Kassette oder CD

enthält alle Hörtexte, die sich im Buch befinden. Das häufige Hören erleichtert Ihnen das Einprägen typisch englischer Redewendungen und wirkt sich positiv auf Ihre Aussprache aus.

Das Lernerhandbuch

ist ein nützliches Nachschlagewerk, das in drei Teilen Hilfen zu Kernfragen des Lernens anbietet: Hilfen also zur Lerntechnik, eine systematische, kurze Englisch-Grammatik und eine Zusammenstellung wichtiger Konversationselemente, die Sie in grundlegenden Gesprächssituationen benötigen.

Wir wünschen Ihnen viel Freude und Erfolg beim Lernen mit **eurolingua English**.

CONTENTS CHART

Grammar	Texts	Learning to learn
..... *das Verb* to be: *Aussageform, Frage, Verneinung und Kurzantworten*		..... *Karteikärtchen zum Einüben von Äußerungen in Alltagssituationen anlegen* ..... *Lerntip: Vokabeln gruppieren*
	..... *englische Werbeslogans*	..... *Erschließungstechniken unbekannter Wörter* ..... *Umgang mit dem Lernerhandbuch*
..... *der bestimmte und der unbestimmte Artikel* ..... *Plural der Nomen* ..... there is / there are ..... *Ortspräpositionen*	..... *englische Wohnungsanzeigen* ..... *Text:* British homes	..... *Vokabeln mit Bildern verbinden* ..... *Vokabeln nach unterschiedlichen Prinzipien ordnen* ..... *zu Vokabeln Zeichnungen anfertigen* ..... *reale Gegenstände beschriften*
..... *die Possessivbegleiter* ..... *der Genitiv mit* s *und* of ..... *einige Verben in der 3. Person Singular (Aussageform)*		..... *eigene Übungen erstellen (Lückentexte)*
..... *der bestimmte und der unbestimmte Artikel* ..... to be ..... *die Possessivbegleiter*	..... *Text:* American homes	
..... this (one) / that (one) ..... these/those	..... *Text:* A letter from America	..... *Vokabeln ordnen* ..... *Karteikarten zu einem Gespräch anlegen* ..... *ein* word map *als Lernhilfe für Vokabeln erstellen* ..... *eigene Übungen zum Lernen der neuen Vokabeln erstellen (Lückentexte)*

Grammar	Texts	Learning to learn
..... *das* present simple: *Aussageform, Frage, Verneinung und Kurzantworten*	..... *Song:* Friday I'm in love (The Cure) ..... *Text:* Schools in Great Britain	..... *Assoziationen zu Vokabeln herstellen*
	..... *englische Gedichte von* Margaret Clark, Eleanor Farjeon, Spike Milligan, Ogden Nash, Annette Wynne u.a.	..... *Worträtsel zu bestimmten Wortfeldern selbst erstellen* ..... *Vokabeln zu Reimpaaren zusammenstellen*
..... *Fragen mit Fragewörtern*	..... Interview with a country musician ..... *Text:* An American family	..... *Vokabeln in unterschiedliche Zusammenhänge bringen (typischer Kontext; Gegensatz; Kausalzusammenhang; chronologische Abfolge; Wortfamilie;* word map) ..... *eigene Übungstexte zum Einüben grammatischer Strukturen schreiben* ..... *nützliche Redewendungen im Unterricht einüben*
..... adverbs of frequency	..... *Text:* Survey of eating habits ..... *Text:* Meals in Great Britain ..... *englische Redewendungen mit* tea *und* cake ..... *Song:* No milk today (Herman's Hermits)	..... *eigenes Übungsmaterial zum Erlernen von neuen Satzstrukturen erstellen* (jumbled sentences)
	..... *Teekarte aus dem Ritz-Hotel* ..... *Rezepte für* afternoon tea: sandwiches and scones	
..... *Mengenangaben:* containers and units ..... how much / how many ..... much / many / a lot of	..... *Song:* Let's have a party (Wanda Jackson)	..... *ein* word map *als Lernhilfe für Vokabeln erstellen*

Grammar	Texts	Learning to learn
..... So/Nor do I; I do too; I don't either; Do you? I don't; Don't you? I do ..... *Objektpronomen* ..... *Wortstellung (Ort vor Zeit)*	..... *Text:* What do they like about Great Britain?	..... *ein* word map *zu einem Text erstellen*
	..... *Dialoge*	..... *aus Dialogen Redemittel zu bestimmten Sprechabsichten heraussuchen*
..... *Verben und Ergänzungen*		..... *Vokabeln pantomimisch darstellen* ..... *Vokabeln nach bestimmten Prinzipien ordnen* ..... *Dialoge zu zweit mit Hilfe der Kassette einüben* ..... *Wortketten bilden* ..... *Vokabeln zu Wortreihen zusammenstellen* ..... *Assoziationen zu Vokabeln herstellen und Begriffe umschreiben*
..... *das* past simple *von* to be *(Aussage, Verneinung und Frage)* ..... *das* past simple *der regelmäßigen und unregelmäßigen Verben (Aussageform)*	..... *verschiedene englische Märchen* ..... *Text:* The little girl and the wolf (James Thurber)	..... *ein* word map *zu Texten erstellen* ..... *Techniken zum Lernen der unregelmäßigen Verben* (nonsense-*Sätze, Reime, Nacherzählen einer Geschichte anhand von Bildern, Visualisieren von Geschichten beim Zuhören)*
..... *das* past simple: *Frage und Verneinung mit* did	..... *Song:* Yesterday (The Beatles) ..... *ein* Peanuts-*Cartoon*	..... *Techniken zum Lernen der unregelmäßigen* past-simple-*Formen mit Hilfe von Mimik, Mnemotechnik, Bildern und Musik*

UNIT 1 : HOW ARE YOU?

.... *sich auf englisch begrüßen*
.... *sich einander vorstellen und nach dem Befinden fragen*
.... *jemanden nach Beruf und Herkunft fragen*
.... *das Verb* to be: *Aussageform, Frage, Verneinung und Kurzantworten*
.... *Lerntips für Vokabeln und Äußerungen in Alltagssituationen; Anlegen von Karteikarten*

1 A visit

1.1 **Sarah Ford, eine Interviewerin für Eurolingua, will Bob, Jane und Jim befragen. Sie trifft sich mit ihnen bei Jane zu Hause. Hören Sie zu. Hat Sarah Ford Jim und Bob schon vorher gekannt?**

1.2 **Hören Sie nochmals zu. Was fehlt im Text? Schreiben Sie die entsprechenden Buchstaben in die Kästchen.**

[a] Pleased to meet you. [b] Fine thanks. [c] How are you? [d] Sarah, this is Bob. [e] Hello, Jim.

2 Introduce somebody

2.1 Spielen Sie das Gespräch in Abschnitt 1.2 zu viert durch.
Dann schließen alle außer „Jane" ihr Buch und spielen auswendig.

2.2 Stellen Sie sich vor, und machen Sie Ihre Nachbarn miteinander bekannt. Verwenden Sie Ihre Vornamen anstelle von A, B und C.

A: Hello. My name is A.
B: Hello. My name is B.
A: B, this is C. C, this is B.
B: Pleased to meet you.
C: Pleased to meet you.

3 First names

Im Englischen ist es viel üblicher als im Deutschen, sich sowohl im privaten als auch beruflichen Bereich beim Vornamen zu nennen. Familiennamen werden meist nur in sehr formellen Situationen verwendet. Es gibt nur eine Anredeform, nämlich you für Sie, du und ihr.

4 Hello and goodbye

Hören Sie zu, und füllen Sie die Lücken. Achten Sie auf die Betonung.

a) Zur Begrüßung sagt man ...

In the morning

In the afternoon

In the evening

b) Wenn man jemandem vorgestellt wird ...

c) Zur Frage nach dem Befinden ...

d) Beim Abschied ...

5 Pronunciation

5.1 [ɪ] oder [i:]? Hören Sie zu, und markieren Sie kurzes [ɪ] wie in Jim oder langes [i:] wie in Jean.

This is a visit. Good evening. Come in. Pleased to meet you, Jean. Jim is busy.

5.2 [ɪ] oder [aɪ]? Hören Sie zu, und markieren Sie die Wörter mit [aɪ] wie in goodbye.

This is nice. Hi, Jim. I'm fine in the morning. Good night. Bye.

6 A meeting

Manuel Gomez, ein Amerikaner, trifft Björn Andersson, einen schwedischen Geschäftspartner, im Hotel. Manuel ist in Begleitung seiner Kollegin Laura Miller und stellt sie Björn vor. Laura verabschiedet sich gleich wieder, weil sie ein Taxi bestellt hat. Was sagen die drei Personen? Spielen Sie das Gespräch ein paarmal zu dritt durch. Wechseln Sie die Rollen.

Manuel begrüßt Björn und fragt nach seinem Befinden.

Björn begrüßt Manuel, antwortet auf seine Frage und fragt nach seinem Befinden.

Manuel antwortet und macht Björn und Laura miteinander bekannt.

Björn begrüßt Laura; er ist erfreut, ihre Bekanntschaft zu machen.

Laura begrüßt Björn und ist ebenfalls erfreut.

Laura erblickt ihr Taxi vor dem Hotel und verabschiedet sich von Björn und Manuel.

Björn verabschiedet sich von Laura. Manuel verabschiedet sich von Laura.

7 What do you do?

7.1 Welche Antworten gehören zu welchen Fragen?

Are you from Germany? [1]
Where's your home now? [2]
Where are you from? [3]
What do you do? [4]

[a] I'm a secretary.
[b] I'm from Frankfurt.
[c] Yes, I am.
[d] It's here in Berlin.

7.2 Hören Sie zu, und prüfen Sie, ob Sie recht hatten.

8 Personal interviews

8.1 Sarah Ford, unsere Interviewerin, befragte Bob, Jane und Jim in Lancaster (England) nach Herkunft und Beruf. Versuchen Sie beim Zuhören, die Tabelle soweit wie möglich auszufüllen.
Diese geografischen Begriffe kommen vor:

Chicago
England
Lancaster
London
Scotland
Wales

In der Zeichnung sind einige neue Wörter illustriert, die Sie hören werden: teacher, painter, doctor, wife, husband, father, mother, parents.

name	job	from	home now
Bob	*teacher*		
Jane			
Jane's father			
Jane's mother			
Jim			
Betty			

8.2 Suchen Sie im Tapescript nach den passenden Informationen. Korrigieren und ergänzen Sie gegebenenfalls Ihre Tabelle. Vergleichen Sie dann mit Ihrem Nachbarn oder Ihrer Nachbarin.

8.3 Was wissen Sie noch über Jim, Bob und Jane? Unterstreichen Sie die richtige Antwort in Satz 2–4, und antworten Sie selbst in Satz 5–8.

1. Is Bob a teacher? — Yes, he is. / No, he isn't.
2. Is Jane from Scotland? — Yes, she is. / No, she isn't.
3. Is Jane's name MacGregor? — Yes, it is. / No, it isn't.
4. Are Jane's parents from Germany? — Yes, they are. / No, they aren't.
5. Is Betty a housewife? ____________________
6. Are Jane and Bob from Lancaster? ____________________
7. Is Jim from Chicago? ____________________
8. Is Jim's wife American? ____________________

8.4 Stellen Sie weitere Fragen. Verwenden Sie die Tabelle unter 8.1.

9 Learning to learn: using flash cards

Fertigen Sie zu bestimmten Alltagssituationen Karteikarten an. Es gibt verschiedene Möglichkeiten.

a) Vorderseite: die Sprechabsicht (auf deutsch)

jemanden begrüßen
– informell
– formell
– morgens/mittags/abends

sich verabschieden
– allgemein
– nachts

Rückseite: die englische(n) Äußerung(en)

Hello. / Hi.
How do you do?
Good morning. / Good afternoon. /
Good evening.

Goodbye. / Bye.
Good night.

b) Vorderseite: die Sprechabsicht (auf deutsch) und die entsprechende Äußerung auf englisch

jemanden nach dem Befinden fragen
How are you?

jemanden vorstellen
Björn, this is Laura.

jemanden nach Herkunft und Beruf fragen

____

Rückseite: die passende Reaktion auf die englische Äußerung

I'm fine, thank you. How are you? /
Fine, thanks. And you?

Hello, Laura. Nice to meet you. /
Pleased to meet you.

____

____

Versuchen Sie, die Kärtchen einem bestimmten, übergeordneten Thema zuzuordnen. Die Sprechabsichten dieser Unit z.B. beziehen sich auf das Thema „kennenlernen". Zu diesem Thema können Sie im Laufe der Zeit weitere Kärtchen mit neuen Sprechabsichten anfertigen.

10 The verb *to be*

10.1 Füllen Sie die folgende Tabelle aus. Sehen Sie gegebenenfalls noch einmal im Tapescript zu Abschnitt 8.1 und in Abschnitt 8.3 nach. Tragen Sie bei der Aussageform und der Verneinung zuerst die *short forms* (abgekürzt) ein. Ergänzen Sie dann die *long forms* (ausgeschrieben).
Vergleichen Sie Ihre fertigen Tabellen mit Ihrem Nachbarn oder Ihrer Nachbarin.

Aussageform

I	'm ______ am ______	from Germany.
You	______ ______	
He She It	______ ______	
We You They	______ ______	

Verneinung

I	'm not ______ am not ______	in England.
You	aren't ______ are not ______	
He She It	______ ______	
We You They	______ ______	

Frage

Where	______	I?
	______	you?
	______	he? she? it?
	______	we? you? they?

Die *short form* braucht man vor allem im gesprochenen Englisch.
Die Verneinung kann auch so gebildet werden: He's not …, You're not … **etc.**

10.2 Setzen Sie die bejahten *short forms* ein. Überprüfen Sie dann anhand der Kassette.

1. "I'______ Swiss, but my wife' ______ English. She'______ from London."

2. "Vienna isn't in Switzerland. It'______ in Austria. It'______ 'Wien' in German."

3. "We'______ from New York. My parents are Scottish. They'______ from Glasgow."

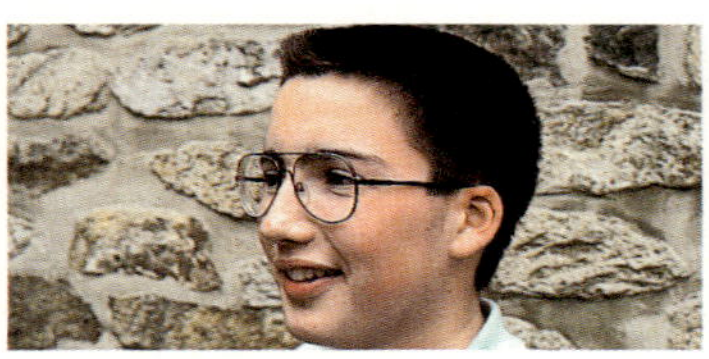

4. "My father'______ Austrian. He'______ from Graz. My mother'______ American."

5. "Herr Möller, you'______ from Berlin. So you'______ German."

6. "We'______ from Dublin. That'______ in Ireland. You'______ not Irish, right?"

10.3 **Hören Sie zu, und setzen Sie dann die *long forms* ein.**

My name ____ Jeff and I ____ a teacher. My wife ____ a secretary. Our home ____ Stuttgart, but we ______ from here. We ____ from Cardiff. Cardiff ____ in Wales. My parents ______ Welsh. They ____ Irish. My mother ____ from Dublin and my father ____ from Northern Ireland. You ____ German, right?

10.4 **Stellen Sie einander Fragen, die mit** ja **oder** nein **beantwortet werden können, und geben Sie die entsprechenden Kurzantworten mit dem Verb** to be**. Kurzantworten werden als höflicher empfunden als ein einfaches** ja **oder** nein**. Verwenden Sie die Satzbautafel. Ergänzen Sie eigene Ideen.**

Is Are	London you Bonn and Mainz ______	in England? in Scotland? ______	Yes,	I am. you are. he is. she is. it is. we are. they are.
Is Are	you your mother your father your parents you and your family ______	English? a doctor / doctors? a teacher / teachers? from Germany? from Innsbruck? ______	No,	I'm not. he isn't / he's not. she isn't / she's not. it isn't / it's not. we aren't / we're not. they aren't / they're not.

11 Who are you?

Schreiben Sie ein paar Sätze über sich selber, etwa so:

Fragen Sie Ihre(n) Kursleiter(in) nach Wörtern, die Sie noch nicht kennen.

My name is Petra. I am a dancer. I am from Austria, but my home is in Germany now. My husband is from the United States. He is a student.

12 England or Britain?

Britain **oder** Great Britain **umfaßt** England, Scotland **und** Wales. **Die offizielle Bezeichnung des Staates lautet** the United Kingdom of Great Britain and Northern Ireland. The British Isles **bestehen aus den Inseln** Britain **und** Ireland.

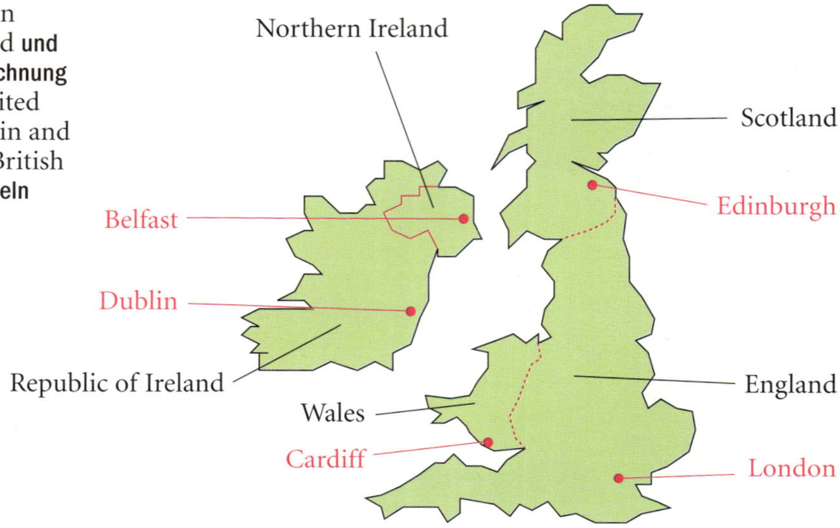

13 Learning to learn: words, words, words

Neue Wörter prägen sich besser ein, wenn man sie in Wortgruppen lernt. Welche Wörter kennen Sie schon zu den Bereichen „Familienmitglieder“, „Berufe“ und „Länder“? Lernen Sie zu den Ländern am besten auch die jeweilige Nationalität:

England – English

Ottos verzweifelter Versuch, seine englischen Vokabeln zu lernen.

UNIT 2: WELCOME TO EUROLINGUA

- .... *angeben, warum man Englisch lernen möchte*
- .... *Englisch in deutschen Werbesprüchen*
- .... *Lerntechniken: Erschließung unbekannter Wörter*
- .... *die Zahlen 1–20*
- .... *Telefonnummern angeben*
- .... *das englische Alphabet: auf Englisch buchstabieren*
- .... *das Eurolingua-System kennenlernen*

1 Why English?

1.1 **Monika, Jürgen und Silke sprechen darüber, warum sie Englisch lernen. Hören Sie zu, und haken Sie die Gründe ab (✔), die genannt werden.**

I want to learn English
☐ for pleasure. ✔
☐ for holidays.

I need English
☐ for my work.
☐ for my studies at school or at university.

I want to ☐ speak English. ☐ read English books. ☐ write English letters.

☐ understand English songs. ☐ watch English films. ☐ listen to English radio.

☐ I have relatives or friends in an English-speaking country.
☐ I want to go to Great Britain or to America on holiday.
☐ I want to meet people from other countries.
☐ I like languages.
☐ I like school.
☐ ______________________________

1.2 **Kreuzen Sie die Antworten an, die auf Sie zutreffen, und ergänzen Sie gegebenenfalls noch weitere Gründe. Fragen Sie Ihre(n) Kursleiter(in) nach neuen Vokabeln. Teilen Sie den anderen Ihre wichtigsten Gründe mit. Welches sind die meistgenannten Gründe Ihrer Gruppe?**

2 English in Germany

2.1 Sehen Sie sich diese englischsprachigen Werbeslogans aus deutschen Zeitschriften an. Für welche Produkte wird geworben? Ordnen Sie zu. Fragen Sie Ihre(n) Kursleiter(in) nach Wörtern, die Sie nicht kennen.

What's the German word for "beauty"?

What's "sky" in German?

1 ☐ Clio. Made in Paradise.

2 ☐ MEN AT WORK.

3 ☐ FEEL AT HOME AT THE OFFICE THE OFFICE OF OUR TIMES.

4 ☐ Try us. Fly us. Business Class

5 ☐ Fall in love with a 597. New and just for women.

6 ☐ A GOOD YEAR FOR RAINY DAYS

7 ☐ THE ESSENCE OF BEAUTY.

8 ☐ It's our business to connect you to yours.

9 ☐ Dressed for action. Boots, shoes, clothing, wind, water, earth and sky.

10 ☐ RUN, CLIMB, JUMP, BEAT, SWEAT, JOG, SWIM, SURF, DRIVE.

a Fluggesellschaft (Iberia)

b Damenjeans (Levi's)

c Herrenkleidung (Hugo Boss)

d Kosmetik (Juvena)

e Wetterfeste Lederjacken (Timberland)

f Kommunikationstechnologie (Siemens)

g Auto (Renault)

h Auto (BMW)

i Büromöbel (Werndl)

j Autoreifen (Goodyear)

2.2 Sehen Sie Zeitschriften nach englischsprachiger Werbung durch, und schreiben Sie diese auf.

2.3 Schreiben Sie fünf Minuten lang englische Wörter und Ausdrücke auf, die im Deutschen in Alltagssituationen verwendet werden. Vergleichen Sie dann mit den anderen Gruppen. Geben Sie sich für jeden Ausdruck, der nicht mehrfach genannt wurde, einen Punkt. Welche Gruppe hat die meisten Punkte?

2.4 Versuchen Sie, die genannten Ausdrücke bestimmten Themen zuzuordnen. In welchen Bereichen gibt es im Deutschen besonders viele englische Wörter?

3 Learning to learn: guessing the meaning of new words

Sie können wahrscheinlich schon mehr Englisch, als Sie selber vermuten. Sehen Sie sich diese Werbeslogans aus englischen Zeitschriften an. Versuchen Sie, so wenig Wörter wie möglich im Vokabelheft nachzuschlagen. Geben Sie dann an, mit welchen der unten genannten Techniken Sie die Bedeutung einiger neuer Wörter erschlossen haben.

– Aus dem Deutschen habe ich abgeleitet: ______________________________

____

– Aus dem Englischen habe ich abgeleitet: ______________________________

____

– Aus dem Zusammenhang habe ich erschlossen: ______________________________

____

– Im Vokabelheft habe ich nachgeschlagen: ______________________________

____

4 Word stress

4.1 Viele englische Wörter sind in ihrem Schriftbild dem Deutschen ähnlich und von daher beim Lesen sofort zu verstehen. Die englische Aussprache allerdings hat einen gewissen „Verfremdungseffekt" zur Folge. Hören Sie zu.

paradise essence quality university welcome civilization generation mineral natural

Diese Wörter haben eine andere Betonung. Welche Silbe wird besonders betont?
Hören Sie nochmals zu, und markieren Sie den Wortakzent, z.B. páradise.
Wo liegt der Wortakzent bei den deutschen Entsprechungen?

4.2 Markieren Sie bei den folgenden Wörtern den Wortakzent.
Überprüfen Sie dann anhand der Kassette, und sprechen Sie die Wörter nach.

●● Éngland ●●● Gérmany ●●●● América

Scotland Ireland Austria Switzerland American evening afternoon holidays parents family husband student teacher personal relatives secretary

5 Numbers and phone numbers

5.1 Hören Sie zu.

1 one	5 five	9 nine	13 thirteen	17 seventeen
2 two	6 six	10 ten	14 fourteen	18 eighteen
3 three	7 seven	11 eleven	15 fifteen	19 nineteen
4 four	8 eight	12 twelve	16 sixteen	20 twenty

5.2 Machen Sie bitte eine Skizze der Sitzordnung im Klassenzimmer, und numerieren Sie die Stühle.

Nun fragen Sie sich gegenseitig:

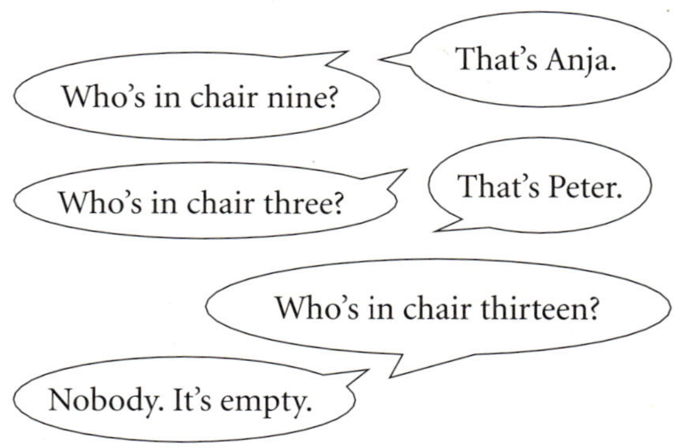

5.3 Diktieren Sie sich gegenseitig ein paar Telefonnummern, die Sie kennen.

7 05 68 88: seven – O – five – six – eight – double eight

6 The alphabet

6.1 Hier sind die Buchstaben nach Lautgruppen sortiert. Hören Sie zu.

A J K   B C D E G P T V   I Y   F S X   L M N   Q U W

Diese Buchstaben bilden keine Lautgruppe: H O R Z

▸▸ **6.2** Sagen Sie das englische Alphabet der Reihe nach auf.
Fangen Sie noch einmal von vorne an, sobald jemand einen Fehler macht.

6.3 Hören Sie zu, und schreiben Sie die entsprechenden Buchstaben auf. Welche Wörter ergeben sich?

6.4 Bilden Sie Dialoge.

A: What's your name?
B: My name is Schlößer.
A: Can you spell that, please?
B: Yes, it's s – c – h – l – o umlaut – double s – e – r

Weitere Fragen:

Where are you from?

What's the name of your street?

Where's your home now?

Can you spell "Eurolingua"?

▸▸ **6.5** Fragen Sie andere im Kurs nach der Schreibweise verschiedener Wörter.

7 Crossword puzzle

Ergänzen Sie die Sätze, und tragen Sie die Wörter unten ein.

I need English for my

________ (2).

I ________ (6)

to ________ (8)

________ (12)

from other countries.

I ________ (6)

to ________ (4)

English letters and

________ (5)

English newspapers.

I ________ (10) English for

________ (7).

I like ________ (1).

In the morning

I ________ (3)

to English radio.

I ________ (9) French

and now I ________ (6)

to ________ (10)

English for

____________ (11).

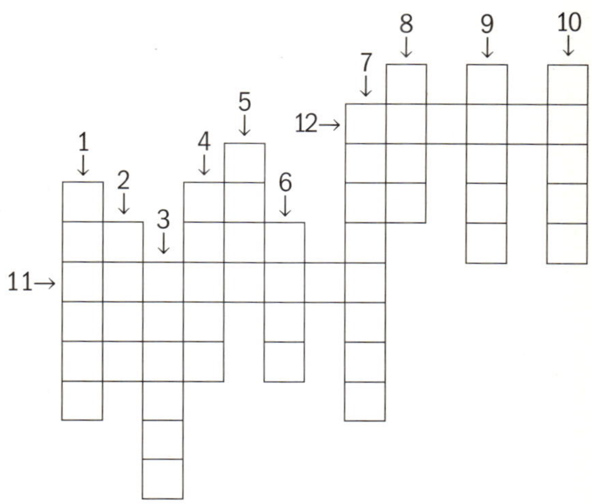

8 Welcome to Eurolingua!

Das folgende Spiel soll Sie mit dem Aufbau des Eurolingua-Systems vertraut machen. Sie brauchen zwei Teams, das Learner's Handbook und das Course Book.

Team A: Names ______________________________

Team B: Names ______________________________

Lösen Sie nun die Aufgaben unter 8.1 und 8.2.

8.1 Arbeiten Sie zunächst mit dem Course Book.

a) Wie lauten die englischen Bezeichnungen dieser Bestandteile Ihres Kursbuches?

1. das Inhaltsverzeichnis ______________________
2. das Vokabular der Units in alphabetischer Reihenfolge ______________________
3. die Texte der Kassettenaufnahmen ______________________
4. die Lösungen zu den Übungen ______________________

b) Auf welcher Seite findet man

1. die Bedeutung des Wortes chair? ____________
2. den Text zur Kassettenaufnahme zu Übung 8 in Unit 3? ____________
3. die Lösungen zu Übung 8.3 in Unit 1? ____________
4. die Inhaltsangaben zu Unit 3? ____________

c) Was bedeuten diese Symbole? Ordnen Sie zu.

Im Lernerhandbuch finden Sie zu unter diesem Stichwort weitere Informationen.	1	a
„Kettenübung": Sie sprechen zu Ihrem Nachbarn bzw. Ihrer Nachbarin, diese(r) wiederum zum nächsten etc.	2	b
Sie arbeiten zu zweit.	3	c
Sie arbeiten zu dritt.	4	d
Sie bilden eine kleine Arbeitsgruppe.	5	e
Die Lösung der Aufgabe steht im Schlüssel.	6	f
Ein Kassettentext wird vorgespielt.	7	g
Die Aufgabe ist schriftlich in Ihrem Heft zu lösen.	8	h

8.2 **Arbeiten Sie jetzt mit dem Learner's Handbook.**

a) Finden Sie die Überschriften für die folgenden drei Hauptteile des Lernerhandbuches:

[A] Lerntechniken ______________________

[B] Sprachgebrauch in Alltagssituationen ______________________

[C] Grammatik ______________________

b) Was gehört in welchen Bereich? Tragen Sie den entsprechenden Buchstaben [A], [B] oder [C] ein.

1. [ ] die Formen des Verbs to be
2. [ ] Ausdrücke, die man zur Begrüßung und zum Abschied braucht
3. [ ] Tips zum Wörterlernen
4. [ ] Redewendungen, die man beim Einkaufen braucht
5. [ ] Techniken zum Erschließen unbekannter Wörter
6. [ ] die Bildung der Pluralform

c) Versuchen Sie, die folgenden Probleme mit Hilfe des Lernerhandbuches zu lösen. Arbeiten Sie mit dem Index am Ende des Lernerhandbuches.

1. Sie möchten einem guten Freund einen englischen Brief schreiben. Wie drücken Sie im Englischen „Lieber Hans" und „Deine Elsa" aus? ______________________
2. Wie warm ist es im Januar in Miami, Florida, wenn dort die Temperatur mit durchschnittlich 68 °F (Fahrenheit) angegeben wird? ______________ °C (Celcius)
3. Kartoffelchips heißen im britischen Englisch crisps. Und im Amerikanischen? ______________________
4. Hosen werden im Amerikanischen mit pants bezeichnet. Wie heißen sie im britischen Englisch? ______________________

8.3 Now check your answers in the Answer Key. Number of correct answers:

Team A ______________________

Team B ______________________

9 What's in a Eurolingua Unit?

Sehen Sie sich die Kurzbeschreibung von Unit 3 auf Seite 26 oben an. Ordnen Sie die verschiedenen Lerninhalte jeweils einem Bereich zu:

[A] Lerntechniken

[B] Sprachgebrauch in Alltagssituationen

[C] Grammatik

Gibt es Lerninhalte, die sich nicht oder nicht eindeutig einem Bereich zuordnen lassen? Welche?

UNIT 3: HOME

.... *das Haus oder die Wohnung beschreiben*
.... *Möbel und Einrichtungsgegenstände benennen*
.... *der bestimmte und der unbestimmte Artikel*
.... *Plural der Nomen*
.... *angeben, was sich wo befindet* (there is / there are; *Ortspräpositionen*)
.... *Techniken zum Vokabellernen für unterschiedliche Lernertypen*
.... *Text:* British homes
.... *englische Wohnungsanzeigen*

1 A living room

1.1 Match the pictures with the words on page 27 and fill in the numbers.

☐ an apple	☐ a computer	☐ a key	☐ a shelf
1 an armchair	☐ a cup and saucer	☐ a lamp	☐ a sofa
☐ a book	☐ a desk	☐ a match	☐ a stereo
☐ a bookcase	☐ an English-German dictionary	☐ a newspaper	☐ a teapot
☐ a bottle	☐ an exercise book	☐ an orange	☐ a telephone
☐ a cat	☐ a fireplace	☐ a pen	☐ a television
☐ a chair	☐ a glass	☐ a photograph	☐ an umbrella
☐ a coffee-table		☐ a plant	☐ a video

1.2 Was bedeuten a bzw. an im Deutschen? Mit welchen Lauten fangen die Wörter an, vor denen an steht?

2 The plural

2.1 Listen to the words in the plural and mark the pronunciation of the ending.

	1	2	3	4	5	6	7	8	9	10	11	12
[z], [s]	x											
[ɪz]												
other												

2.2 Fill in the missing forms of the singular or plural.

book	books	______	bookcases
cat	______	______	oranges
chair	______	______	glasses
lamp	______	______	matches
photograph	______	______	shelves
telephone	______	child	______

2.3 Hören Sie noch einmal die Kassette zu Abschnitt 2.1 an, und ordnen Sie die Wörter nach ihren Endungen: [s] bzw. [z] oder [ɪz]. Schreiben Sie die Wörter in zwei Spalten in Ihr Heft.
Welche Endlaute haben die Wörter im Singular, bei denen man die Pluralendung [ɪz] ausspricht?

2.4 Ergänzen Sie die Regeln für die Pluralbildung, und schreiben Sie Beispiele auf.

1. Beim regelmäßigen Plural wird an das Wort ein ______ angehängt, z.B. bei ______________ .

2. Wenn das Wort auf -s oder -ch endet, wird ______ angehängt, z.B. bei ______________ .

3. Wörter, die auf Konsonant + y enden, haben im Plural die Endung -ies, z.B. dictionary → dictionaries

   oder ______________ .

4. Einige Wörter haben eine unregelmäßige Pluralform, z.B. ______________ .

3 What is there in the living room?

Describe the picture of the living room on page 26.

There is a television. There are two cats.

4 The definite article

4.1 Listen and underline the [ðɪ].

1. the sofas
2. the table
3. the orange
4. the television
5. the umbrella
6. the cats
7. the apple
8. the dictionary
9. the English dictionary
10. the newspaper
11. the American newspaper
12. the German newspaper

4.2 Vor Wörtern mit welchen Anlauten spricht man the [ðɪ] aus?

5 Where is the cat?

5.1 Complete.

The cat is on the chair. ____________

It is under ____________

in front of ____________

behind ____________

next to ____________

between ____________

5.2 Ask questions about the living room on page 26.

A: Where are the photos?
B: They're on the shelf. … Where is the umbrella?
C: It's behind the armchair. … Where is … ?

6 Pronunciation

6.1 **[æ] und [e]: Hören Sie zu. Welche der Wörter werden mit [æ] gesprochen wie** cat **und welche mit [e] wie** ten? **Ordnen Sie die Wörter in Ihrem Heft in zwei Spalten unter dem entsprechenden Laut ein.**

6.2 **Der Laut [eɪ]: Unterstreichen Sie die Wörter, die mit [eɪ] wie in** name **gesprochen werden. Überprüfen Sie dann anhand der Kassette.**

name cat table America and radio can Jane family Wales apple have stay they am eight

6.3 **[v] und [w]: Hören Sie zu, und sprechen Sie nach.**

[v] have television verb relatives video My relatives have a television and a video.
[w] we where want what work Wales word one We want to work. Where is Wales?

7 Learning to learn: words, words, words

Sehen Sie sich die folgenden Techniken zum Vokabellernen an, und suchen Sie sich die aus, die Ihnen am meisten zusagt.

7.1 **Neue Wörter prägen sich gut über das Auge ein, z.B. durch beschriftete Zeichnungen.**

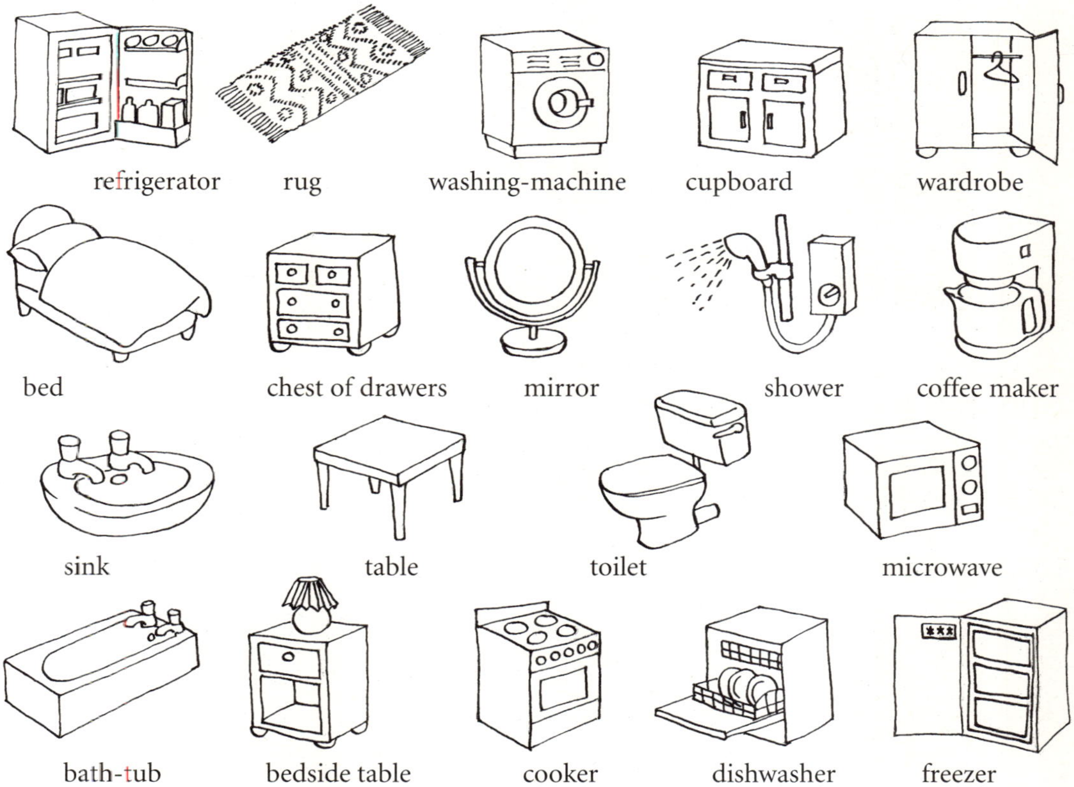

Wenn Sie mit Karteikärtchen lernen, können Sie auf die eine Seite den entsprechenden Gegenstand zeichnen und auf die andere Seite das englische Wort schreiben.

7.2 Lernen Sie neue Wörter, indem Sie sie zu bestimmten Gruppen zusammenfassen:

a) Versuchen Sie, die neuen Wörter aus Abschnitt 1.1 – soweit möglich – den folgenden Bereichen zuzuordnen:

- Möbel (furniture)
- Gegenstände des täglichen Gebrauches (things for daily use)

b) Ordnen Sie die neuen Möbelstücke aus Abschnitt 7.1 bestimmten Räumen zu:

bedroom

____

____

____

____

kitchen

____

____

____

____

bathroom

____

____

____

____

c) Fassen Sie alle Gegenstände in Ihrer Wohnung zusammen, die Sie „hören" oder „riechen" können:

7.3 Auch das eigene Tun kann die Merkfähigkeit beim Vokabellernen unterstützen.

a) Richten Sie einen Raum dieses Hauses ein, indem Sie selbst die Gegenstände hineinzeichnen. Beschreiben Sie dann auswendig, was sich in Ihrem Raum befindet.

In my bathroom there is a bath-tub, a sink …

b) Beschriften Sie kleine Zettel, und kleben Sie sie zu Hause an die entsprechenden Gegenstände.

c) Haben Sie Probleme mit der Schreibung neuer Wörter? Schauen Sie sich ein Wort genau an, schließen Sie dann die Augen, und schreiben Sie es ganz groß in die Luft.

8 A study

Look at the picture and listen. Which description is right: a, b or c?

9 British homes

Read the text and listen.

In Britain, about eighty per cent of people live in houses and only about twenty per cent live in flats. About sixty-four per cent of people own their houses or flats. Most other people live in council houses and pay rent to local authorities. Only about ten per cent rent from private landlords.

There are three main types of houses in Britain:

terraced houses

semi-detached house

detached house

10 Flats in London

10.1 Sehen Sie sich diese Wohnungsanzeigen aus der englischen Zeitung The Times an.

Wie lauten die Abkürzungen für diese Begriffe?

balcony
bathroom
bedroom
dining room Eßzimmer
fitted eingebaut
flat
fully-fitted kitchen komplette Einbauküche
furnished möbliert
garage
house
kitchen
large groß
living room
luxury
near in der Nähe von
per week pro Woche
reception room Wohnzimmer
separate
shower
studio apartment Einzimmerwohnung
unfurnished unmöbliert

REGENTS PARK Nr Zoo Lge 2 bed, 1 bath flat, shwr room, ff kit, recep, din rm, unfurn. £200 pw. 0171 436 8685.

WHITEHALL Near Parliament Large luxury 3 bed flat, 2 bath, fit kit, reception/dining rm, furnished/unfurnished. £350 pw. 0171 723 4455.

CHELSEA studio apt with sep kit & bath. £125 pw. 0171 731 8798.

HAMPSTEAD
Attractive house,
3 bedrooms with fitted wardrobes,
2 bathrooms,
new fully-fitted kitchen,
living room with fireplace,
dining room with large balcony, garage.
£560 pw.
0171 433 1609.

KENSINGTON
Lge hse, 3 bed, bath,
2 receps, din rm.
£195 pw.
0171 371 1201.

KNIGHTSBRIDGE
Near Harrods
Lux 4 bed flt, 2 bath, liv rm,
ff kit, balc, gge, furn/unfurn.
£650 per week.
0171 638 3848.

10.2 What's the best house or flat for the Brown family?
Mr and Mrs Brown have two children and can pay two hundred pounds per week in rent.

10.3 Geben Sie selbst eine kleine Annonce für eine Wohnung in Ihrer Stadt auf englisch auf.

UNIT 4: FAMILY

.... *Verwandtschaftsbeziehungen erläutern*
.... *Besitzverhältnisse ausdrücken*
.... *die Possessivbegleiter:* my, your, his *etc.; der Genitiv mit* s *und* of
.... *Lerntechnik: eigene Übungen erstellen (Lückentexte)*
.... *einige Verben in der 3. Person Singular (Aussageform)*

1 Lynn's family

1.1 Sarah Ford schaut sich die Photos in Lynns Wohnzimmer an und stellt Fragen dazu. Decken Sie den Text unter 1.2 ab, und hören Sie zu. Schauen Sie dabei die beiden Photos an. Schreiben Sie die drei fehlenden Namen zu der jeweiligen Person.

_________ _________ Anne _________ Sharon Jack

1.2 Listen again and read the two conversations.

a)
Sarah: Is this you and your husband?
Lynn: Yes, that's right.
Sarah: Is your husband English?
Lynn: No, he isn't.
Sarah: Where is he from?
Lynn: He's from Canada. He's a pilot. He works for British Airways.
Sarah: What's his name?
Lynn: Robert.
Sarah: Where are you?
Lynn: On holiday in Scotland, at my parents' house. We're in their garden.
Sarah: It looks very nice.
Lynn: Oh, yes. It is great. We go there every summer.
Sarah: Is this your daughter?
Lynn: Yes, that's our daughter. Her name's Anne. Our son, Andrew, isn't in the photo.
Sarah: How old are your children?
Lynn: Andrew's twelve and Anne's seventeen. She wants to go to university in Germany. Sometimes she speaks German with our neighbours here in London. They're from Berlin.

b)
Sarah: Who's this?
Lynn: That's my brother Jack with his daughter, Sharon.
Sarah: How old is she?
Lynn: She's five. She starts school this year.
Sarah: Is this her mother?
Lynn: No, that's Jack's girlfriend, Maria. Jack's divorced.
Sarah: Where are they?
Lynn: Here they are at their house in California.
Sarah: Your brother lives in California?
Lynn: Yes, in Santa Barbara. He works for an American computer firm. He's a computer programmer.
Sarah: What's the name of the firm?
Lynn: Its name's Microdisk, I think. He likes his job very much.
Sarah: That's nice.

1.3 **Read the text. Underline the wrong parts.**

Lynn lives in New York. Every year she goes to Canada on holiday. Her children have a house there. Its garden is very nice.

Lynn's husband is from Austria. His name is Robert. He is a computer programmer for British Airways.

Lynn has a son in California. His name is Jack. His daughter's name is Sharon. She is fifteen. Jack works for an American airline. Its name is Microdisk.

Lynn has a brother and a sister. Their names are Andrew and Anne. Anne speaks French and wants to go to university in Germany.

Lynn and Robert's neighbours are German. They're from Salzburg, but they live in England now.

1.4 **Now write the correct sentences:** Lynn lives in London.

2 Possessive adjectives, genitive with *s* and *of*

2.1 **Lesen Sie die zwei Gespräche unter Abschnitt 1.2 noch einmal durch.**
Wie heißen die folgenden Ausdrücke auf englisch bzw. auf deutsch?

dein Mann / Ihr Mann → ____________

____________ ← deine Tochter / Ihre Tochter / eure Tochter

mein Bruder → ____________

sein Name → ____________

unser Sohn → ____________

____________ ← her name

____________ ← its name

____________ ← their garden

2.2 **Ordnen Sie die** *possessive adjectives* **den entsprechenden** *personal pronouns* **zu.**

I	you	he	she	it	we	they
my	______	______	______	______	______	______

2.3 **Suchen Sie aus Abschnitt 1.2 und 1.3 die englischen Entsprechungen dieser Ausdrücke heraus, und vervollständigen Sie die Regeln. Vergleichen Sie mit Ihrem Nachbarn oder Ihrer Nachbarin.**

Lynns Ehemann ____________________

Jacks Freundin ____________________

der Name seiner Tochter ____________________

Lynns und Roberts Nachbarn ____________________

das Haus meiner Eltern ____________________

Den Genitiv mit s **verwendet man für**

____

der Name der Firma ____________________

Den Genitiv mit of **verwendet man für**

____

3 Practice

3.1 **Ask questions about the people in the photos on page 33.**

A: Who's this?
B: That's Robert.

A: Who's Robert?
B: He's Lynn's husband.
or: He's Anne and Andrew's father.

3.2 **Combine words from the two lists and make questions.**

What's the president's name?
What's the name of the hotel?

List 1
the president
the hotel
your teacher
the restaurant
her friend
your father
his parents
the computer firm

List 2
name
telephone number
address

3.3 **Who's this? What's that? Complete the answers.**

1. That's Lynn's husband.
2. That's Lynn's brother.
3. That's Lynn's son.
4. That's Lynn's daughter.
5. That's the computer firm where Jack works.
6. That's Jack's daughter.
7. That's Jack's girlfriend.
8. That's Lynn and Robert's children.
9. That's Anne and Andrew's parents.
10. That's the airline for which Robert works.

His Her Its	name is …
Their names are …	

3.4 **Complete.**

"_____ sister's name is Lynn. _____ husband is from Canada. _____ name is Robert. Lynn and Robert have two children. _____ names are Anne and Andrew."

4 Learning to learn: do-it-yourself English (gaps)

a) Erstellen Sie Ihre eigenen Übungen. Schreiben Sie ein paar Sätze aus der Perspektive einer der Personen auf den Photos von Seite 33 oder über Ihre eigene Familie, und verwenden Sie so viele *possessive adjectives* wie möglich.

Anne:
My parents' names are Lynn and Robert. I have a brother. His name is Andrew …

b) Schreiben Sie Ihre Sätze dann als Lückentext, indem Sie die *possessive adjectives* weglassen. Tauschen Sie Ihre Lückentexte aus.

5 Verbs in the third person singular *(he, she, it)*

Read again the texts in sections 1.2 and 1.3 and underline all verbs after he, she and it (third person singular). Then complete the table.

I / you / we / they		he / she / it	
work	live	______	______
look	like	______	______
want	go	______	______
speak	have	______	______
start	be	______	______

6 Talking about photos

6.1 Suchen Sie aus einer Zeitschrift ein Photo mit mehreren Personen aus. Denken Sie sich zu den Personen ein paar Einzelheiten aus, und machen Sie sich Notizen (Namen? Beziehung zueinander? Nationalität? Wohnort?).

6.2 Zeigen Sie sich gegenseitig Ihre Photos: Notieren Sie sich Fragen, die Sie zu den anderen Photos stellen können. Verwenden Sie

Who's …?	What are …?
Who are …?	Where's …?
What's …?	Where are …?

Sprechen Sie dann über die Photos.

6.3 Write about your photo.

The woman in the picture is Claudia. She lives in Leipzig.
The man's name is Marco.
He is Claudia's boyfriend. Claudia has two children …

6.4 Legen Sie alle Beschreibungen auf einen Stapel. Ziehen Sie einen Zettel. Welches Bild wird darauf beschrieben?

7 A letter from Canada

Andrew verbringt seine Ferien bei seinen Großeltern in Canada.
Er schreibt einer Freundin in England diesen Brief.
Ergänzen Sie die passenden Verben, und überprüfen Sie dann anhand der Kassette.

~~be~~ be be be be be be be be come have have have have like like live want want work

Dear Cindy,

How ___are___ you? I ________ fine. I ________ on holiday in Canada. I ________ it here. There ________ lots of things to do here and I ________ very little time to write. This week my cousin Caroline ________ here. She ________ eleven. She ________ in Toronto. She ________ here every summer. She ________ very nice. Next year she ________ to go to London on holiday.

My grandparents ________ a very nice house. It ________ a wonderful garden. Granddad ________ the garden too. He ________ there every day. Granny ________ two cats. Their names ________ Mungojerrie and Rumpelteazer. Caroline ________ here. We ________ to go to the swimming-pool.

Love, *Andy*

CN Tower in Toronto

8 Pronunciation

8.1 Listen and repeat the sentences. Then check the Tapescript and find the words with short [ʌ] as in but and long [ɑː] as in glass. Write the words in two lists in your exercise book.

8.2 Listen and repeat the sentences. Then check the Tapescript and find the words with [ʃ] and [tʃ] as in short and teacher and with [ʒ] and [dʒ] as in television and German. Write the words in four lists in your exercise book.

8.3 [r] and [l]: Listen and repeat.

Where is her friend? The bottle is on the table. The children like school. There are three trees in the garden. That's right.

Option 1: FURTHER PRACTICE

.... *Übungen zur Wiederholung (bestimmter und unbestimmter Artikel,* to be, *Possessivbegleiter, Vokabular, Aussprache)*
.... *Text:* American homes

1 The definite and indefinite articles

1.1 Say these words with a **or** an. **Then listen and check.**

bar milkshake hamburger taxi interview film star American film star T-shirt
clown manager English manager mountain bike yoghurt inter-city English film
ticket baseball university Austrian university party cocktail hobby old hobby

1.2 Sehen Sie sich noch einmal die internationalen Wörter an, die Sie in Unit 2 unter Abschnitt 2.3 gesammelt haben. Suchen Sie die Substantive heraus, und lesen Sie sie mit the [ðə] **oder** the [ðɪ] **vor.**

2 Right or wrong?

Make dialogues.

A: London is in England.
B: Yes, it is.

B: We are in a hotel.
A: No, we aren't.

1. My name is Elvis.
2. There's a cat on the table.
3. Your mother is from Austria.
4. Lynn and Robert are Swiss.
5. I'm German.
6. Salzburg is in Austria.
7. You're a man.
8. I'm five years old.
9. You're a woman.
10. There's a sofa in this room.
11. We are good students.
12. Mickey Mouse is American.
13. There are ten people here.
14. Your husband is a teacher.
15. Our teacher is English.
16. There are tables and chairs in the classroom.
17. We are on holiday.
18. New York and Chicago are in Scotland.
19. ____________________
20. ____________________

3 Is this a dog?

3.1 Write the answers.

Is this a dog?

No, this isn't a dog.
This is a cat.

1. Is he a pilot?

2. Are there three televisions in the picture?

3. Are you the teacher?

4. Is this Ireland?

5. Is the car from England?

6. Are they in the United States?

7. Is she in the living room?

3.2 Schreiben Sie nun selber zu diesen Bildern Fragen auf, die eine verneinte Antwort erfordern. Geben Sie sie dann jemandem in der Klasse zum Richtigstellen.

1

2

3

4

5

4 Who are they?

4.1 Complete the text.

name:
Julia O'Connor
from:
Ireland
home now:
Bristol,
England
job:
teacher, housewife
husband: David
husband's job: computer programmer – American firm in Bristol
children: Oliver (7) and Lisa (9)
likes: computers, languages (German)
next holiday: Scotland

Julia O'Connor ______ from Ireland. She lives in ___________ in England now. She ______ a teacher and a housewife. ______ husband's name ______ David. He'______ a computer programmer. He ___________ for an American firm in Bristol. Julia and David ___________ two children. ______ names are Oliver and Lisa. They ______ 7 and 9 years old. Julia ___________ computers and languages. She speaks ___________ . She ___________ to go to ___________ for her next holiday.

4.2 Write about the people in the photos.

1.

name: Mark Rogers
from: Kansas, United States
home now: Toronto, Canada
job: teacher
children: Tommy (15)
likes: holidays, good restaurants
next holiday: California

2.

5 What are the questions?

5.1 Fill in the questions.

Sarah: ______________________________

Lynn: That's my son.

Sarah: ______________________________

Lynn: Andrew.

Sarah: ______________________________

Lynn: He's twelve.

Sarah: ______________________________

Lynn: Here he is at his grandparents' house in Canada.

5.2 Arbeiten Sie mit einem der beiden Dialoge aus Unit 4 unter Abschnitt 1.2. Schreiben Sie Lynns Antworten auf, und lassen Sie Platz für Sarahs Fragen. Versuchen Sie dann, die Fragen aus dem Gedächtnis zu ergänzen.

6 The same, but different

6.1 Welche *possessive adjectives* klingen wie diese *short forms* von to be?

it's ________ you're ________ he's ________ they're ________

6.2 Fill in the gaps.

1. The Smiths have a large house. _______ new.
2. Sarah: _______ American, right? What's _______ name?

3. Sally has a brother. _______ name is Kevin. _______ a student.
4. Mr and Mrs Sedlmair live in Germany but _______ Austrian. They live with _______ daughter in Frankfurt.

7 Words, words, words

7.1 Find the partners.

ask answer chair children coffee cup daughter evening friend garden glass go house husband listen pen paper parents partner radio read saucer sister son speak table tea television wife write

THINGS (7x)	PEOPLE (5x)	VERBS (4x)	TIME (1x)
bottle and …	brother and …	come and …	morning and …

7.2 **Combine words from the two lists.**

to write	a book
to understand	English
to spell	a flat
to speak	a house
to read	a language
to own	a letter
to live in	a newspaper
to listen to	a question
to learn	the radio
to ask	a song
	your teacher
	a word

8 Pronunciation

8.1 **Listen and repeat.**

1. can balcony address that tape glass match have page garden make has start table after lamp are
2. he spell English be twelve she French then England well every hotel bed next eleven check we between desk repeat
3. film like write six pilot picture with night morning children child fill in dialogue time think nine right live thing five
4. my very goodbye family balcony why twenty empty

8.2 **What is the pronunciation of the letters** a, e, i **and** y**? Write the words from 8.1 in the right list. Then listen and check.**

1. a
   - [æ] can
   - [eɪ] tape
   - [ɑː] glass
2. e
   - [e] spell
   - [iː] he
3. i
   - [ɪ] film
   - [aɪ] like
4. y
   - [ɪ] very
   - [aɪ] my

9 American homes

Read the text and listen. Match the people with their homes.

About sixty-six per cent of Americans own their homes. About seventy per cent live in houses, twenty-five per cent in apartments and three per cent in mobile homes (or trailers) in mobile home parks (or trailer parks).

1 We live in a nice old house with a porch in the front and a big yard in the back. In the summer we sit on the porch in the evening and talk with the neighbors. It's nice to have a backyard because the children can play there. Sometimes, on the weekend, we have a barbecue in our backyard.

2 My husband and I live in a trailer park in Florida. We like it because we can have our own home and it's not expensive. We love the warm weather here. In our trailer park there is a swimming-pool and a club house with a laundry room.

3 I am single and live in a condo in Greenwood Apartments right in the middle of town. There is a swimming-pool, a club room and a tennis court. The apartment buildings are large, with about twelve apartments in one building.

VOCABULARY

backyard Garten hinter dem Haus
barbecue Grillparty
because weil
big groß
building Gebäude
condo = condominium Eigentumswohnung
expensive teuer
in the back hinten
laundry room Wäscheraum
middle of town Stadtmitte
mobile home Wohnwagen
own eigene(r,s)
to play spielen
porch Veranda
right direkt
single ledig
to sit sitzen
tennis court Tennisplatz
trailer Wohnwagen
weather Wetter
weekend Wochenende
yard Garten

UNIT 5: AT THE MARKET

.... *Obst und Gemüse einkaufen*
.... *Zahlen ab 21*
.... *Anrede in Geschäften in Großbritannien*
.... *bitten und danken im Englischen*
.... *Eigenschaften benennen (Adjektive)*
.... this (one) / that (one); these / those
.... *Lerntechniken: Karteikärtchen zu einem Gespräch anlegen; Vokabeln zu* word maps *zusammenstellen; eigene Übungen zum Erlernen des neuen Vokabulars erstellen*
.... *Text:* A letter from America

1 The apples are sixty pence a pound

1.1 **Listen and fill in the missing prices.**

1.2 **Make dialogues.** A: One pound of apples, please.
B: That's sixty pence. … Four oranges and a melon, please.
C: That's one pound eighty. …

2 At the market

2.1 Peter Wilson lebt in Nordengland. Er geht auf dem Markt einkaufen. Eine ältere Frau bedient ihn. Decken Sie den Text unter 2.2 ab, und hören Sie zu: Was kauft Peter? Wie nennt ihn die Frau?

2.2 Now listen again and read the text.

Assistant: Yes, love?
Peter: Can I have a pound of apples, please?
Assistant: These, love?
Peter: Yes, that's right.
Assistant: Anything else?
Peter: Yes please, four oranges.
Assistant: Anything else?
Peter: That's all, thanks.
Assistant: Here you are then.
Peter: How much is that?
Assistant: One pound sixty, please.
Peter: … er … Here you are.
Assistant: Thanks, love. Next, please.
Peter: Cheerio. Thank you.
Assistant: Thanks, love. Bye.

2.3 Spielen Sie den Dialog. Versuchen Sie, den Tonfall so gut wie möglich nachzuahmen.

3 Love at the shops?

In Großbritannien ist es durchaus üblich, daß das Verkaufspersonal die Kunden und Kundinnen mit Kosenamen anspricht. Diese sind je nach Landesteil verschieden. Wohl am meisten hört man love, dear und duck oder ducky. Man hört sie vor allem in kleinen Läden und auf dem Markt. Die familiäre Anrede erleichtert den persönlichen Kontakt. In vornehmen und teuren Geschäften oder in Banken wird man hingegen mit sir oder madam angesprochen.

4 Words, words, words

What colour are they? Match the fruits and vegetables with a colour.

red tomatoes ____________
____
____

green ____________
____
____

yellow ____________
____
____

orange ____________
____
____

blue ____________
____

brown ____________
____

white ____________
____

5 Shopping: useful phrases

5.1 **Read the dialogue in section 2.2 again and try to complete the following phrases. Check your answers with a neighbour.**

1. etwas verlangen

Yes, please?

________ a pound of apples, please?

Yes, certainly. Anything else?

Yes ________ , four oranges.

2. nach dem Preis fragen

________ that?

80p.

________ the mushrooms?

3. sagen, daß man nichts mehr möchte

Anything else?

No, thanks, ________ .

Here you are.
One pound ten, please.

5.2 **Legen Sie Karteikärtchen zum Thema** shopping **an. Schreiben Sie auf die Vorderseite die deutsche Sprechabsicht (z. B.** etwas verlangen**) oder den deutschen Ausdruck (z.B.** Nein danke, das wär's.**) und auf die Rückseite die jeweiligen englischen Ausdrücke (z. B.** Can I have …? **oder** No thanks, that's all.**). Fertigen Sie sowohl Kärtchen für die Rolle des Verkäufers als auch des Käufers an. Numerieren Sie die Kärtchen, und üben Sie ein Verkaufsgespräch mit einem Partner: Jeder von Ihnen übernimmt dabei eine Rolle. Versuchen Sie, von den deutschen Vorgaben auszugehen. Wechseln Sie die Rollen.**

6 At the newsagent's

Make dialogues between a newsagent and his customers. Use the phrases from section 5. Reverse roles.

an evening newspaper

TV Times

a packet of cigarettes

a box of matches

a phonecard

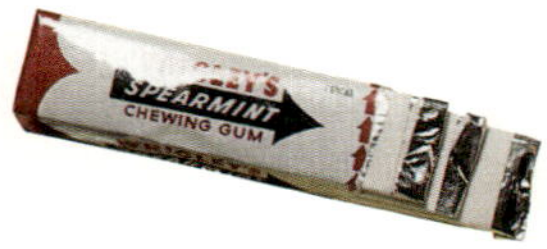

a packet of chewing-gum

7 *Please* and *thank you*

7.1 Please verwendet man im Englischen, wenn man eine Bitte äußert, aber auch, um ein Verbot auszudrücken.

7.2 Um zu danken und auf Dank zu reagieren, gibt es verschiedene Möglichkeiten.

Thanks **ist persönlicher als** thank you. **Als Antwort auf** thanks **oder** thank you **darf keinesfalls das deutsche** bitte **mit** please **übersetzt werden.**

7.3 **Hören Sie die Minidialoge unter Abschnitt 7.2 auf der Kassette. Gehen Sie dann im Kursraum herum und geben Sie einer anderen Person etwas (ein Buch, Kugelschreiber etc.). Verwenden Sie dabei die Ausdrücke aus Abschnitt 7.2, und versuchen Sie, den Tonfall so gut wie möglich nachzuahmen.**

8 Numbers

8.1 **Listen and repeat.** 2–20 3–30 4–40 5–50 16–60 17–70 18–80 19–90

8.2 **Write down the numbers.** 21 twenty-one 642 six hundred and forty-two

Then listen and check. 32 43 54 65 76 87 98 100 150 375 500 999

8.3 **Listen and fill in the prices.**

9 What's this? Who's that?

9.1 Look at these pictures.

This oder that? Ergänzen Sie die Regeln:

– Für Dinge und Personen, die sich nahe beim Sprechenden befinden, verwendet man __________ .

– Für Dinge und Personen, die etwas weiter weg sind, verwendet man __________ .

9.2 Wie heißen die verschiedenen Personen und Gegenstände in Ihrem Klassenzimmer? Fragen Sie Ihre(n) Kursleiter(in) oder andere Teilnehmer(innen). Verwenden Sie this und that.

9.3 Schreiben Sie die neuen Wörter auf. Fertigen Sie als Lernhilfe ein word map zum Thema classroom an.

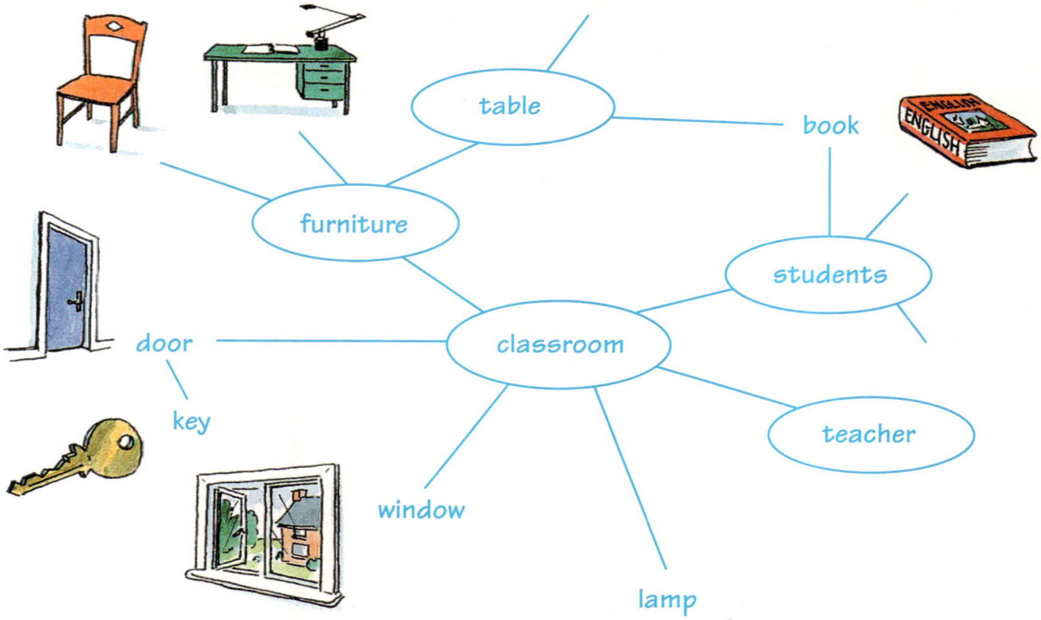

10 *This one or that one? These or those?*

10.1 **Listen and fill in** this one, that one, these **or** those.

Assistant: Yes, please?

Peter: How much are ________ mushrooms?

Assistant: 25 p a quarter. But they're not very good.

Peter: Oh?

Assistant: No, they're old. ________ mushrooms over there are fresh. They're 35 p a quarter.

Peter: Well, can I have a quarter of ________ mushrooms, please?

Assistant: Here you are. Anything else?

Peter: Yes, a melon, please.

Assistant: ____________ ?

Peter: Yes, ____________'s all right.

Peter: And two pounds of potatoes, please.

Assistant: Two pounds of potatoes. Yes, sir. ________ here?

Peter: Yes, ________ are fine. That's all.

10.2 **Wann verwendet man** one **nach** this **und** that?

Wie lauten die Pluralformen? this / this one – ________________ that / that one – ____________

10.3 **Complete** this/these … (here) – that/those … (there).

1. ________ oranges here are fresh.
2. ________ potatoes there are old.
3. ________ pineapple here is £1.20.
   ________ one there is £1.50.
4. How much are ________ apples here?
   And ________ over there?
5. How much are ________ bananas there?
6. ________ man here is Harry Brown.
7. ________ woman there is his wife, Jackie.
8. Who are ________ people here?
9. Who's ________ man next to Joe over there?

11 How are the melons different?

11.1 Match the adjectives with the pictures.

~~cold~~ interesting long full cheap new bad small small

11.2 Bilden Sie Dialoge, und zeigen Sie dabei auf den entsprechenden Gegenstand.

A: How are the drinks different?
B: This one's hot and that one's cold. … How are the bottles different?
A: These are full and those are empty. … etc.

12 Pronunciation

12.1 Try to say the words from the list with the right stress: ●•• or •●•

alphabet apartment apricot balcony banana cigarette cucumber customer exercise expensive family furniture interesting newsagent photograph potato president raspberry restaurant strawberry telephone tomato umbrella vegetable

12.2 Then listen and check. Mark the stress on difficult words: álphabet

13 A letter from America

Pictures from Maine

13.1 **Read this letter and listen. Find and underline the American words for** holiday – flat – favourite – garden – centre – cinema – theatre – shop – a shop where you can buy medicine, cosmetics, snacks and drinks

Dear Brigitte,

Thanks very much for your long letter and the wonderful photos of your family. It's very interesting for me to read about your life in Germany.

This week Bob and I are on vacation at our new beachhouse in York, a small town on the coast of Maine. We love our new house. It's a nice change from our apartment in Boston. It's a great house, 75 years old. It's not very big, but it has three bedrooms and six people can sleep in it. When you and Günter come to Boston in the summer, we can all come up here for a week. Behind the house there is a big yard with lots of apple and pear trees. Now I can make Bob's favorite dessert, apple pie, with apples from our yard. Bob wants to plant some vegetables too.

But I want to tell you about York. York is famous for its houses from the 18th century. There is an American Indian museum too. In the summer a lot of tourists come to York because there is a nice, long beach where you can lie in the sun or take a walk. You can swim in the sea, but the water is very cold. Sometimes Bob and I go to a small seafood restaurant near the beach. It is not very expensive and the food is very good. You can get a whole lobster for only $ 6.95.

From York it's only 7 miles to the town of Kittery. In Kittery there is a large shopping center with restaurants (not only fast food!), movie theaters, supermarkets, drugstores, department stores etc. In America most stores open at 9 or 10 o'clock in the morning and close at 9 or 10 in the evening. Some restaurants and supermarkets are open 24 hours a day, 7 days a week. Sometimes Bob and I go to the supermarket in the middle of the night. It's fun because there aren't many people there then.

I hope you and your family are fine. I can't wait to see you soon! Regards to Günter.

Love,

Valery

13.2 True or false? Correct the false sentences.

1. Bob and Valery live in York.
2. They have a holiday home in Boston.
3. York is a small town on the coast of Maine.
4. A lot of tourists come to York in the winter.
5. Bob and Valery do their shopping in Kittery.
6. Some supermarkets in Kittery are open 24 hours.

13.3 Talk about your town. You can use these expressions:

I / We	live in ________ .	

That's a	small / large	town in the	east / west / south / north	of Germany.

In ________	there is	a ________		where you can ________ .
	there are	some / a lot of	________	

________	is famous for its	________ .
	has a / some / a lot of	________ .

13.4 Answer Valery's letter. Talk about your town, your family and your home.

14 Learning to learn: do-it-yourself English (gaps)

Erstellen Sie eigene Lückentexte zum Einüben der neuen Vokabeln. Sie können dazu Sätze aus dem Buch oder eigene Sätze mit neuen Wörtern verwenden. Auslassen können Sie z. B. die neuen Wörter oder alle Verben oder jedes fünfte, sechste oder siebte Wort.

Hier ist ein Beispiel aus dieser Unit:

In the summer a lot of tourists ______ to York because there ______ a nice,
long beach where you ______ ______ in the sun or ______ a walk.
You ______ ______ in the sea, but the water ______ very cold. Sometimes
Bob and I ______ to a small seafood restaurant near the beach.

In the summer a lot ______ tourists come to York because ______ is a nice,
long beach ______ you can lie in the ______ or take a walk. You ______
swim in the sea, but ______ water is very cold. Sometimes ______ and I go
to a ______ seafood restaurant near the beach.

Sie können die einzusetzenden Wörter auch ungeordnet unter den Text schreiben. Legen Sie den Lückentext ein oder zwei Tage auf die Seite, bevor Sie sich selbst testen.

UNIT 6: ROUTINES AND HABITS

.... *das* present simple: *Aussageform, Frage und Verneinung*
.... *über Gewohnheiten sprechen und nach Gewohnheiten fragen*
.... *Uhrzeit*
.... *Wochentage*
.... *Song:* Friday I'm in love (The Cure)
.... *Text:* Schools in Britain

1 This is William

1.1 William ist der Held einer beliebten englischen Buchserie von Richmal Crompton. Hören Sie zu.

1. My name is William because my father is the son of William Shakespeare.
2. School finishes for me when I'm 16. That's 12 years at school. Ugh!
3. My father drinks 30 bottles of whisky every day. Then he goes to work.
4. I go to school at 9 o'clock and I come home at 4 o'clock.

5. My mother cooks old boots for breakfast.
6. I'm 16 years old.
7. I'm not very good at school.
8. I have 3 pet tigers. They sleep in my bed.
9. I wear these clothes to school.
10. I speak 15 languages.

1.2 Welche seiner Aussagen halten Sie für wahr (true) **und welche für eine Übertreibung** (a tall story)**?**

We think number one is true / a tall story. We think numbers … and … are tall stories.

2 William says …

Fill in the correct forms of the verbs.

be be be be come cook drink finish go go have ~~say~~ sleep speak wear

William __says__ his father ____________ the son of William Shakespeare. He ____________ school when he ____________ sixteen. His father ____________ 30 bottles of whisky before he ____________ to work. William ____________ to school at 9 o'clock and ____________ home at 4 o'clock. His mother ____________ old boots for breakfast. He ____________ not very good at school. He ____________ three pet tigers. They ____________ in his bed when he ____________ . He ____________ those clothes to school. He ____________ 15 languages.

3 The present simple: verbs in the third person singular

3.1 Listen and mark the pronunciation of the ending:
[s] as in he drinks, [z] as in she comes or [ɪz] as in it finishes.

	1	2	3	4	5	6	7	8	9	10	11	12	13	14	15	16
[s]	x															
[z]		x														
[ɪz]																

3.2 Make three lists: [s], [z] and [ɪz]. Listen to the tape for section 3.1 again and write the verbs in the right list.

3.3 Versuchen Sie, eine Regel für die Aussprache des -s in der 3. Person abzuleiten:

– [s] spricht man nach ______________________

– [z] spricht man nach ______________________

3.4 Schreibung: Für die s-Form der 3. Person Singular gelten die gleichen Regeln wie für das Plural-s.
Schreiben Sie die folgenden Verben in der 3. Person:

to read → he __________

to listen → she __________

to come → it __________

to write → he __________

to sleep → she __________

to drink → he __________

to stay → it __________

to use → she __________

to watch → he __________

to finish → it __________

to miss → she __________

to match → it __________

Ausnahmen

to go → he / she / it __________

to have → he / she / it __________

to be → he / she / it __________

can → he / she / it ______ start

4 Tell a tall story

4.1 Schreiben Sie ein paar wahre und unwahre Sätze über sich, Ihre Familie oder weitere Personen auf, und übertreiben Sie manchmal dabei. Versuchen Sie es mit folgenden Verben:

cook drink be (am, are, is) wear sleep go want have can start work finish work come home watch television

4.2 Tauschen Sie Ihre Sätze aus. Jeder soll herausfinden, welche Aussagen wahr und welche übertrieben sind.

5 Do they like school?

5.1 **Sarah Ford talks to Diana (12) and Steven (10) about school. First, listen to the interview with Diana. Does she like school?**

5.2 **Now listen again and complete the text.**

Sarah: What time do you get up, Diana? 

Diana: Half past ________. I have my breakfast in the car.

Sarah: You start school at ________ o'clock, then? 

Diana: Yes. Well, ________ to ________. 

Sarah: Do you like school?

Diana: It's OK. School meals are disgusting. And I hate the uniform.

Sarah: Ah, you wear a uniform. What time do you finish?

Diana: A quarter to ________. 

Underline the correct answer.

1. Does Diana get up at half past eight? — Yes, she does. / No, she doesn't.
2. Does school start at ten? — Yes, it does. / No, it doesn't.
3. Does she have breakfast at home? — Yes, she does. / No, she doesn't.
4. Do Diana's parents have a car? — Yes, they do. / No, they don't.

5.3 **Read the interview with Steven and fill in these verbs. Then listen and check.**

do do go go help like play think watch

Sarah: Do you ________ school, Steven?

Steven: No, I ________ it's boring.

Sarah: What do you ________ at the weekend?

Steven: Well, on Saturdays I ________ football.

Sarah: And on Sundays?

Steven: I ________ my dad in the garden or ________ TV. Then I ________ my homework.

Sarah: When do you ________ to bed?

Steven: At nine o'clock. But on Fridays and Saturdays I ________ to bed at ten because there isn't school the next day.

Now answer these questions.

1. Does Steven like school? — No, he …
2. What does he do on Saturdays?
3. Does he help his father on Sundays?
4. When does he go to bed on Sundays?
5. Does he go to bed at nine o'clock on Fridays?
6. Do his parents have a television?

5.4 **Bewerten Sie folgende Aussagen mit** That's true. / That's false. / I don't know. **Stellen Sie die falschen Aussagen richtig.**

1. Diana doesn't like school meals.
2. She doesn't start school at nine o'clock.
3. She wears jeans and a sweatshirt to school.
4. Her parents don't have a car.
5. Steven doesn't like school.
6. His friends don't watch television.
7. He does his homework on Sundays.
8. He plays rugby at school.

5.5 **Schreiben Sie weitere Aussagen über Diana und Steven auf, die Sie einer anderen Person aus dem Kurs zur Beurteilung geben.**

6 Questions, short answers and negatives

Complete the table. Fill in I, you, he, she, it, we, they.

Questions / Short answers

Questions			Short answers					
Do	______ ______ ______ ______	go to school?	Yes,	______ ______ ______ ______	do.	No,	______ ______ ______ ______	don't.
Does	______ ______ ______	speak English?	Yes,	______ ______ ______	does.	No,	______ ______ ______	doesn't.

Negatives

______ ______ ______ ______	don't (do not)	go to school.
______ ______ ______	doesn't (does not)	speak English.

7 A pronunciation game

7.1 Read these sentences aloud.
Then listen and check.
What's Jean's secret?

Jean likes tea, but she doesn't like breakfast.
She likes jeans, but she doesn't like sweatshirts.
She likes east, but she doesn't like west.
She likes Dean. Does she like Ben?

7.2 Bilden Sie ähnliche Sätze.
Hier sind ein paar Ideen: Willy mag nur Wörter mit Doppelbuchstaben, Susan nur Wörter, die mit S beginnen, Ágatha nur Wörter, die auf der 1. Silbe betont werden, Joe nur einsilbige Wörter ...
Lesen Sie Ihre Sätze vor, und lassen Sie die anderen raten, nach welchem Prinzip Sie vorgegangen sind.

8 What people do

8.1 Match the expressions with the pictures.
Write down two more activities.

1. ☐ drink beer
2. ☐ drive a car
3. ☐ wear glasses
4. ☐ play rugby
5. ☐ eat meat
6. ☐ ride a bicycle
7. ☐ smoke a pipe
8. ☐ speak French
9. ☐ talk in your sleep
10. ☐ sing in the shower
11. ☐ ______________
    ____
12. ☐ ______________
    ____

8.2 Ask questions about the pictures.

A: Do you eat meat?
B: Yes, I do.
C: Do you drink beer?
D: No, I don't. … etc.

▸▸ **8.3** Ask questions and give short answers.

	you	live	in Germany?
	your grandparents	work	in Buckingham Palace?
	the Queen	sleep	on the sofa?
	the President of the United States	watch television	in the White House?
Do	you and your family	play football	in a park?
Does	we	speak English	at home?
	your cat	drink beer	in a pub?
	your best friend	eat pizza	in a French restaurant?
	______________	______________	______________
	______________	______________	______________

8.4 Write about two other people (yourself, your grandmother ...).
Write only negative sentences about one person.

My name isn't William. I don't live in England. I don't play rugby.
My grandmother lives in Passau. She drives a car and rides a bicycle.

9 The days of the week

9.1 Listen to the song and fill in the days of the week.

Friday I'm in love (The Cure)

I don't care if ______________'s blue

______________'s grey and ______________ too

______________ I don't care about you

It's ______________ I'm in love

______________ you can fall apart

______________ break my heart

______________ doesn't even start

It's ______________ I'm in love

______________ wait

and ______________ always comes too late

but ______________ never hesitate ...

VOCABULARY 1 I don't care if ... mir ist es egal, ob ...; blue blau, melancholisch; 2 grey grau, trüb; 3 I don't care about you ... du bist mir egal; 5 to fall apart auseinanderfallen; 6 heart Herz; 7 not even nicht einmal; 10 too late zu spät; 11 never nie; to hesitate zögern

9.2 What colours does the singer of the song associate with Monday, Tuesday and Wednesday? What do you think? What colour are the other days of the week for the singer?

What colours do you associate with the days of the week? Why?

Some more colours: pink purple black

10 What time is it?

10.1 Say the times.

3.30: It's half past three.
9.45: It's a quarter to ten.

12.15	1.05	10.50	6.25	4.45	9.20	7.35
8.10	5.40	2.10	11.55	12.00	3.45	8.30

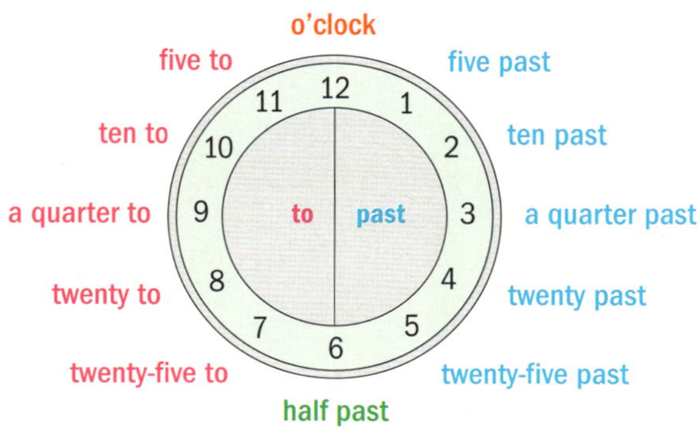

Big Ben in London

10.2 Complete the clocks and practise with a partner.

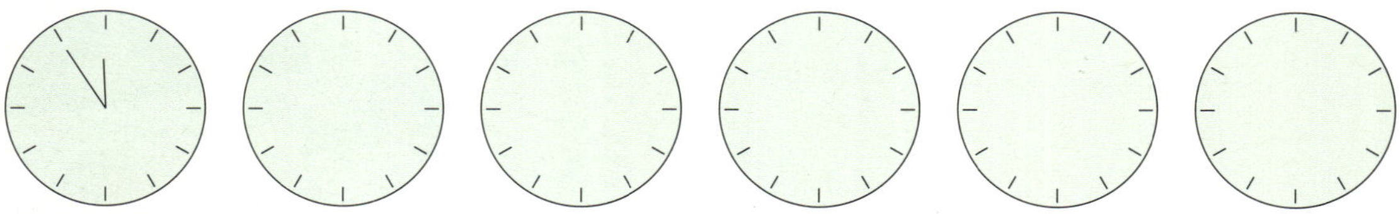

A: What time is it? B: It's five to twelve.

10.3 Say the times with in the morning, in the afternoon, in the evening, at night.

am = from 0.00 to 12.00
pm = from 12.00 to 24.00

3.30 pm 11.00 am 1.05 pm 2.15 am 6.35 am
10.45 pm 5.55 am 12.45 pm 12.25 am

The 0° longitude passes through Greenwich, a district of southeast London.

10.4 In winter, standard British time is Greenwich Mean Time (GMT). It is one hour behind Central European Time. From March to October there is British Summer Time. It is one hour ahead of GMT.

10.5 **Fill in** at, in **or** on.

______ Monday Diana gets up ______ half past eight ______ the morning and goes to school. She has lunch ______ twelve o'clock and she comes home ______ a quarter to four ______ the afternoon. She comes home ______ five o'clock ______ Wednesday because she plays tennis. ______ Saturday and Sunday she stays at home and watches TV ______ the evening. She goes to bed ______ eleven o'clock ______ night.

11 Schools in Britain

Listen and read. Then answer the questions.

In Britain children start school when they are five years old. For seven years they go to a primary school. At the age of eleven they go to a secondary school where they must stay until they are sixteen. Secondary school can be a comprehensive school, which about 90% of all schoolchildren attend, or a grammar school.
Outside the state school system Britain has private independent schools. Independent schools are called public schools, but they are not really public because they are very expensive.
For British children the school day lasts from nine to four. They eat lunch at the school canteen. A lot of schools in Britain still have uniforms.

1. When do children start school in Britain?
2. How old are they when they go to a secondary school?
3. At what age do they finish secondary school?
4. What secondary schools are there in Britain?
5. Why are public schools not really public?
6. What do many British children wear to school?
7. When does the school day start?
8. When does it finish?

Eton, a famous public school near Windsor

A comprehensive school in London

Option 2: POEMS AND PUZZLES

.... *Gedichte und Worträtsel*

1 Time for a poem

Listen to these poems. Then read the poems aloud.

Rain
There are holes in the sky
Where the rain gets in,
But they're ever so small
That's why rain is thin.
Spike Milligan

Water
I like the water in a cup,
I like it in the sea,
I even like the dripping rain
When it can't rain on me!
Margaret Clark

The House Cat
The house cat sits
And smiles and sings
He knows a lot
Of secret things.
Annette Wynne

The Kitten
The trouble with a kitten is
THAT
Eventually it becomes a
CAT.
Ogden Nash

August Heat
In August when the days are hot,
I like to find a shady spot,
And hardly move a single bit
And sit –
And sit –
And sit!
Anonymous

VOCABULARY rain Regen; hole Loch; sky Himmel; to get in hereinkommen; ever so small ganz klein; that's why deshalb; thin dünn ■ even sogar; dripping tropfend; to rain regnen ■ to sit sitzen; to smile lächeln; secret geheim ■ kitten Kätzchen; trouble Problem; that daß; eventually schließlich; to become werden ■ August heat Augusthitze; shady spot schattiger Platz; hardly kaum; to move sich bewegen; a single bit ein klein bißchen

Blue is the Sea
Blue is the sea
Green is the grass
White are the clouds
As they slowly pass.
Black are the crows
Brown are the trees,
Red are the sails
Of a ship in the breeze.
Anonymous

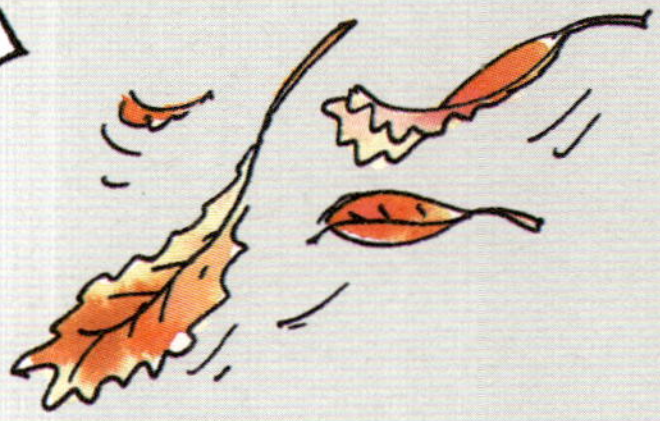

Down! Down!
Yellow and brown
The leaves are falling over the town.
Eleanor Farjeon

VOCABULARY cloud Wolke; as während; slow(ly) langsam; to pass vorüberziehen; crow Krähe; sail Segel; ship Schiff; breeze Briese
■ down herunter; leaf, *pl.* leaves Blatt, *pl.* Laub; … are falling fallen; over über

2 Rhymes

2.1 Which words sound the same? Find ten pairs.

a lot – all – beach  – beautiful – bed  – beer  – blue – 
boring – brother – to buy – bye – cat – cheese  – cold – day – dear – to drink – to eat –
flat – to go – here – hi! – hot – how – interesting – to know – long – meat 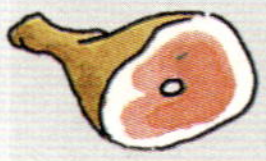 – to meet –
men – mother – night  – no – now – old – pea 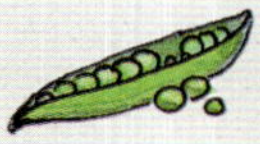 – peach  –
pear 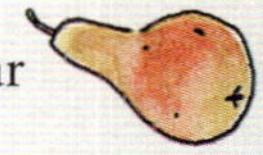 – pen  – pie  – pink  – to play – potato 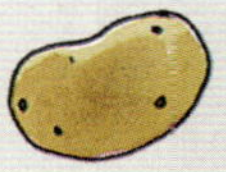 –
red  – right – to say – sea – to see – to sing  – sink – small – son – song –
sun  – to stay – tall – there – these – thing – to think – tomato  – true –
useful – to wear – white – window  – wonderful – wrong – year – yellow

2.2 Try to write a poem with four lines. Read it to the class.

3 Crossword puzzle

What are these things from a kitchen?

Across

1. You can sit on it.
2. You can make coffee with it.
3. You wash the vegetables in it.
4. You cook on it.
5. There is frozen food in it.
6. You sit at it when you eat.
7. The cups, glasses etc. are in it.
8. You prepare food in it when you don't have much time.

Down

9. ______________________
(Find your own definition.)

4 Jumble puzzle

You can eat these things. What are they?

Complete the proverb with the circled letters.

A	N	N	A	A	B	
E	G	R	A	N	O	
E	S	C	H	E	E	
C	K	N	E	I	C	H
L	E	P	A	P		
T	O	O	P	A	T	

Don't put all your eggs in one _ _ _ _ _ _.

5 Hidden words

In this square there are ten numbers. Where are they? Words can go across or down.

T	W	E	L	V	E	S	U	N
D	F	G	K	L	P	I	W	E
C	X	Z	T	I	Y	X	G	I
S	E	V	E	N	Y	N	T	G
F	S	W	N	G	K	S	W	H
O	Z	D	R	G	J	I	O	T
U	W	A	B	H	J	X	L	Y
R	Q	F	O	N	E	T	N	D
F	I	V	E	H	J	Y	X	A

6 Missing words

Fill in the correct forms of the verbs.

1. William ____________ a uniform at school.
2. Diana ______________ home at four o'clock.
3. On Saturday Steven ____________ football.
4. William ______________ French.
5. William's father ______________ work at five o'clock.
6. Diana ______________ her school uniform.
7. She ____________ until half past eight in the morning.
8. In the evening Steven __________ television.

Now fill in the verbs. Which word goes across?

7 Make your own puzzles

Stellen Sie nun selbst ähnliche Rätsel her, und tauschen Sie sie im Kurs aus.
Hier einige Ideen für mögliche Wörter:

days of the week furniture things in the classroom family fruit and vegetables verbs adjectives places

Wenn Sie ein jumble puzzle machen, können Sie das Lösungswort in einen Satz aus einer alltäglichen Situation eintragen lassen. Wenn Sie wollen, können Sie die Situation zeichnen.

UNIT 7: QUESTION TIME

.... *Fragen mit Fragewörtern* (who, what, which, when, where, why, how)
.... *bei Verständnisschwierigkeiten im Unterricht nachfragen*
.... *Lerntechniken: Vokabeln in verschiedenen Zusammenhängen lernen; eigene Übungstexte schreiben*
.... *ein Ratespiel zu Units 1–7*

1 An interview with a country musician

1.1 This is the first part of an interview with Rickie Williams. Find the answers. Then listen and check.

1. ☐ Who writes the songs in your group?
2. ☐ What instruments do you play?
3. ☐ Who's your favourite musician?
4. ☐ Who do you prefer?
5. ☐ What's the name of your new album?
6. ☐ Which song on your new album do you like best?

a We write the songs together. First the other members write the music and then I write the lyrics.
b I like all the songs. But "Days without you" is my favourite.
c The name is "Tennessee Dreams".
d I play the guitar and the banjo. And I sing, of course.
e I think I prefer Elvis.
f My favourite musicians are Elvis Presley and Beethoven.

1.2 Here are the answers to the second part of the interview. Make up the questions. Then listen and check.

g Our new album comes out next week.
h I live in Atlanta, but I want to move to Nashville, Tennessee, soon.
i Our record company is in Nashville, and the other band members live there too.
j My wife? She's our manager.
k Jonny is seven and Patsy eleven years old.
l Oh, they like my music very much. Sometimes they come to our concerts.

1.3 Sehen Sie sich die Fragen in Abschnitt 1.1 an, und versuchen Sie, die Verwendung der Fragewörter who, what **und** which **zu ermitteln. Ergänzen Sie dann die Regeln.**

1. Who bedeutet auf deutsch _______ und _______ .

   – Wenn who = _______ verwendet man in der Frage keine Umschreibung mit do/does.

2. What und which haben vor *Nomen* eine ähnliche Bedeutung: _____________ , _____________ .

   – Bei der Frage nach einer beschränkten Zahl von Dingen oder Personen verwendet man _________ .

   – Bei der Frage nach einer nicht beschränkten Zahl verwendet man _________ .

2 An American family

2.1 Read and listen.

Jim and Annie Taylor live in Orlando, Florida with their two children. Jim is a hotel manager. He works at Disney World. He likes his job very much because he meets lots of interesting people. Annie is a secretary. She works part-time at a lawyer's office. The children go to school. They are 10 and 13 years old. This is a typical day for the Taylor family: Annie wakes up at 6.30. She gets up and makes breakfast. At 7 she wakes Jim and the children. They all have breakfast in the kitchen. At 7.30 Jim goes to work. At 8.30 Annie drives the children to school because their school is near her office. Annie finishes work at 3 o'clock in the afternoon. At 3.15 she fetches the children from school. On their way home they stop at a supermarket and buy food for supper. At home the children do their homework and Annie prepares supper. At 5.30 Jim comes home from work. At 6 the Taylors have supper. The children go to bed at 8 o'clock. Then Annie and Jim watch the news and a film on television. They go to bed at 11.

2.2 Form questions about the text. Use different question words.

Who ...?

Where ...? When ...? What ...? Why ...? How ...?

Collect your questions on a piece of paper, like this:

Where ...	What ...	Who ... (wer?)	Who ... (wen?)	When ...	Why ...	How ...
do Jim and Annie live?	does Jim do?	gets up at 6.30?				

2.3 Ask the other students some of your questions about the text.

3 Learning to learn: do-it-yourself English (practice texts)

3.1 Schreiben Sie einen kurzen Text über eine Phantasie-Familie. Sie können den Text über Jim und Annie Taylor als Vorlage benutzen. Unterstreichen Sie in Ihrem Text einige Satzteile, nach denen man mit Where ...? When ...? What ...? Why ...? Who ...? How ...? fragen kann.

Kurt and Jutta Becker live <u>in Essen</u> with their three children. <u>Kurt</u> gets up <u>at 7 in the morning</u> and wakes <u>the children</u>. ...

3.2 Arbeiten Sie dann mit einer anderen Gruppe, und tauschen Sie Ihre Texte aus. Stellen Sie jeweils Fragen zu dem fremden Text. Die Verfasser versuchen, auswendig zu antworten.

4 Interview another student

4.1 Stellen Sie Fragen zusammen, die Sie jemandem aus dem Kurs stellen möchten.

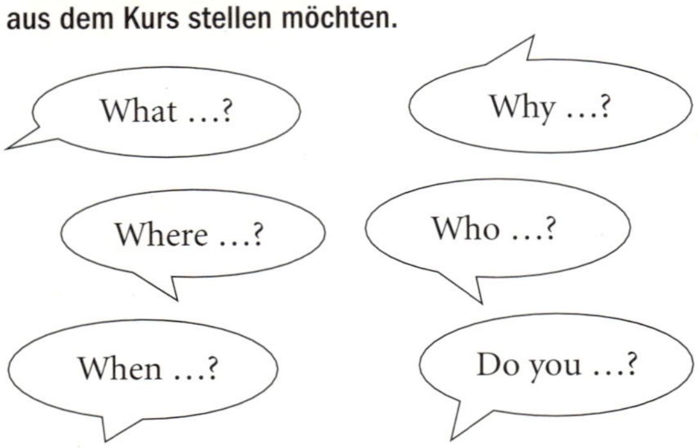

Mögliche Themen:

4.2 Interviewen Sie sich nun gegenseitig. Machen Sie sich als Interviewer Notizen zu den Antworten Ihres Interviewpartners, und berichten Sie dann der ganzen Gruppe.

Sabine is a taxi driver. She likes her work because it is interesting. She meets lots of nice people. She gets up at 7 and starts work at 8. …

5 If you don't know, ask!

5.1 Was sagen Sie in den folgenden Unterrichtssituationen? Ordnen Sie die Äußerungen auf Seite 69 zu.

1. Sie fragen, wie ein bestimmtes Wort oder Ausdruck auf englisch oder deutsch heißt: ☐ ☐ ☐ ☐ ☐
2. Sie verstehen etwas nicht: ☐ ☐ ☐
3. Sie fragen, wie ein bestimmtes Wort geschrieben wird: ☐ ☐
4. Sie möchten wissen, ob das, was Sie gesagt oder geschrieben haben, korrekt ist: ☐
5. Sie fragen, wie man ein bestimmtes englisches Wort ausspricht: ☐
6. Sie wissen etwas nicht: ☐
7. Sie fragen, wie man ein bestimmtes Wort in einem Satz verwendet: ☐
8. Sie fragen nach, ob man Sie verstanden hat: ☐

Legen Sie sich Karteikärtchen zum Thema „Unterrichtswortschatz" an.

5.2 Verwenden Sie einige der Fragen in 5.1, um möglichst viel über die abgebildeten Dinge herauszufinden, und fragen Sie Ihre(n) Kursleiter(in). Erstellen Sie eine Liste wie unten angegeben.

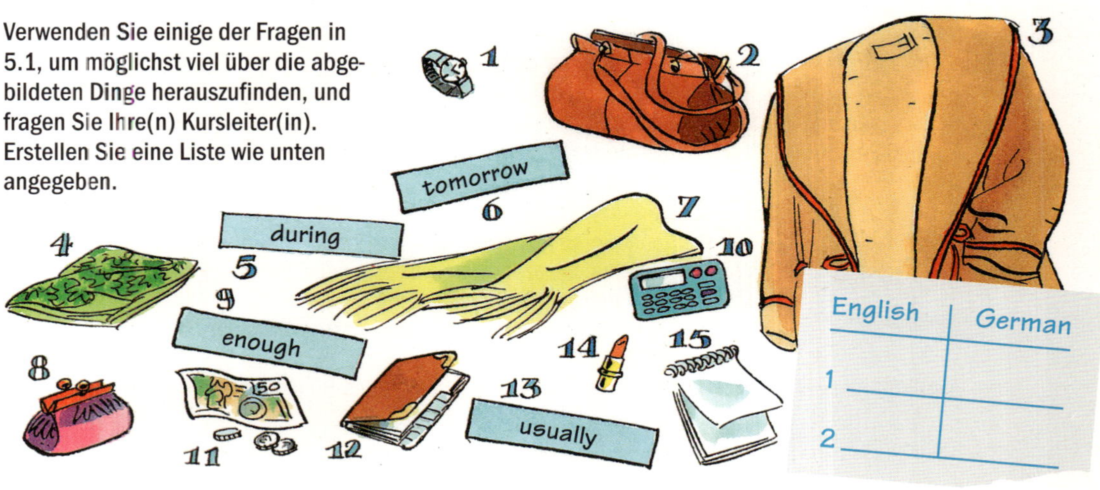

6 Learning to learn: vocabulary

6.1 Lernen Sie neue Wörter nicht isoliert, sondern immer in irgendeinem Zusammenhang. In welchen Zusammenhängen stehen die folgenden Wörter?

a) get up

1. What time do you get up? She gets up at 7 in the morning.
2. get up – go to bed
3. wake up – get up – make breakfast – go to work
4.

b) news

1. I watch the news on television.
2. news – new – newsagent – newspaper
3.

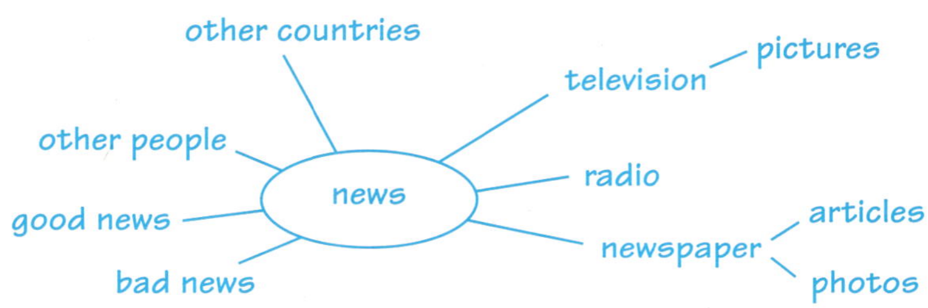

6.2 Versuchen Sie, neue Wörter Ihrer Wahl aus Unit 6 und 7 in jeweils mindestens zwei verschiedene Zusammenhänge zu bringen. Vergleichen Sie mit Ihrem Nachbarn oder Ihrer Nachbarin.

7 A board game: Test your English

Sie brauchen:

- das Spielfeld auf S. 114/115
- Spielfiguren und Würfel für 4–6 Personen

- die Aufgaben auf S. 71

Spielregeln

1. Würfeln Sie der Reihe nach, und rücken Sie die gewürfelte Anzahl Punkte vor.
2. Wer auf einem Aufgabenfeld ankommt, wählt zuerst einen Assistenten oder eine Assistentin und dann eine Aufgabennummer. Die lange Fassung des Spiels umfaßt 50 Aufgaben (rote und blaue Nummern). Sie können aber auch eine Kurzvariante spielen und nur die Aufgaben 1–25 mit den roten Nummern lösen.
3. Zu zweit wird dann die Aufgabe unter der jeweiligen Nummer gelöst. Aufgepaßt: Die Nummer muß ausgewählt werden, bevor man die Aufgabe kennt.
4. Wenn die Aufgabe erfüllt ist, kontrollieren die anderen anhand des Schlüssels. Für jede richtige Antwort gibt es einen Punkt, maximal also 4 Punkte. Die Punkte erhält der Spieler, der gewürfelt hat.
5. Jede gelöste Aufgabe wird durchgestrichen und darf nicht nochmals gewählt werden.
6. Gewonnen hat, wer am Schluß des Spiels die meisten Punkte hat.

1. What colour are these vegetables?
tomatoes, carrots, potatoes

2. Ask another student about his or her job.
3. Ask a question about each picture.
4. *83 99 33 17*
5. An American: How are you?
You: [?]

6. An Englishman: How do you do?
You: [?]
7. Susan: Hello, I'm Susan.
You: [?]
8. What is there in your living room?
Say 4 things.

9. *14 40 18 80*
10. Say 4 drinks.

11. 8.25 am 4.15 pm 6.30 pm 11.00 pm
12. Ask another student about his or her home.
13. Say 4 fruits.

14. I am [?] secretary.

15. We live [?] Stuttgart.
16. 7.55 am 8.35 pm 3.45 pm 1.20 am
17. Where are you from?
18. I work [?] a lawyer's office.
19. Say you do not do the things in the picture.
20. Say the activity for each picture.
21. You: [?]
Your teacher: "opposite" means "Gegenteil" in German.
22. Where is your home now?
23. *37 41 19 90*
24. You: [?]
Your teacher: It's B-R-E-A-K-F-A-S-T.
25. He doesn't work [?] Mondays.

26. What time do you get up?

27. What is there in your kitchen? Say 4 things.

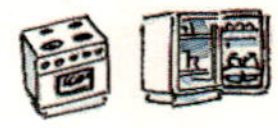

28. Ask another student about his or her family.
29. Ask another student about his or her hobbies.
30. An Englishwoman: Thank you very much.
You: [?]

31. You <u>make</u> breakfast, but you [?] your homework.

32. What is there in your handbag or briefcase (Aktentasche)? Say 4 things.
33. What are the missing words?
mother – father
[?] – brother
wife – [?]
[?] – son
34. Assistant: Yes, love?
You: [?]

35. What's your phone number?
36. You: [?]
Assistant: They're 80 p a pound.
37. How do you spell your name?
38. Say 3 green vegetables.

39. My husband comes home [?] work [?] 5 o'clock [?] the afternoon.
40. Our children go [?] school.
41. What do you do every day? Say 4 things.
42. Assistant: Anything else?
You: No, [?]
43. Assistant: Here you are.
You: [?]
44. They do [?] homework [?] home.
45. What don't you do? Say 4 things.
46. What do you do at the weekend?
47. You <u>ride</u> a bicycle, but you [?] a car.

48. What time do you go to bed?
49. What is the opposite (Gegenteil) of these words? expensive – full – old – long
50. Ask another student about his or her routines and habits.

UNIT 8: FOOD AND DRINK

- .... *über Eßgewohnheiten sprechen*
- .... adverbs of frequency
- .... *Texte:* Survey of eating habits *und* Meals in Britain
- .... *Lerntechnik: eigenes Übungsmaterial erstellen* (jumbled sentences)
- .... *englische Redewendungen mit* tea *und* cake
- .... Song: No milk today (Herman's Hermits)

1 Breakfast in Britain

Match the words with the pictures. Check the Vocabulary Book if necessary, or ask your teacher.

Full English breakfast

Continental breakfast

☐ bacon	☐ fried egg	☐ orange juice	☐ sausage
☐ bread	☐ honey	☐ pepper	☐ sugar
☐ butter	☐ jam	☐ porridge	☐ tea
☐ cereal	☐ marmalade	☐ rolls	☐ toast
☐ coffee	☐ milk	☐ salt	☐ tomato

2 Eating habits in Britain

2.1 Read this newspaper article. Then listen to the tape and read the text again.

Survey of Eating Habits

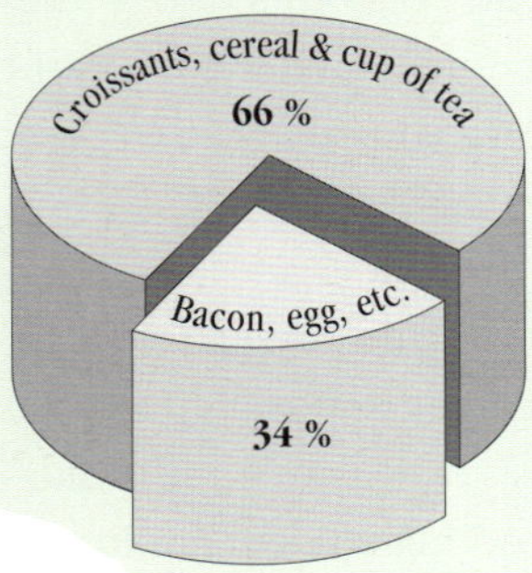

A new survey of eating habits of adults in Britain shows big changes in what and how we eat. Most people never eat a traditional English breakfast of bacon and eggs. Sixty-six per cent of adults say that they usually start their day with continental-type breakfast of only cereal and toast. But most people always have a cup of tea with milk in the morning. Other interesting facts to come from the survey are:

* 50 % of adults have only one full meal a day.
* Their main meal is supper: it's usually at half past five or 6 o'clock.
* 66 % eat four or more snacks a day.
* For snacks they eat sandwiches, bread and butter, cake, crisps, fruit and biscuits.
* 50 % drink half a litre of milk a day; they normally drink full-cream milk.
* 70 % drink 6 or more cups of tea or coffee a day.

2.2 **True or false? Correct the false statements.**

1. Most people in Britain always have a traditional English breakfast.
2. Their main meal is lunch at 12 or 1 o'clock.
3. Supper is usually at half past five or 6 o'clock.
4. Milk is a very popular drink in Britain.
5. Most people usually drink full-cream milk.
6. People in Britain eat a lot of snacks.
7. Most people drink one cup of tea or coffee a day.

3 Are they typical?

3.1 **Sarah Ford talks to some people about their eating habits.**

chocolate biscuit

chocolates

Listen and fill in the chart.
You will hear these new words: often, occasionally, rarely.

	What do you normally have for breakfast?	What's your main meal?	What snacks do you eat between meals?
1. John 	porridge or muesli, toast, tea		
2. Sue 			
3. Mary 			

3.2 **Look at the newspaper article again and say whether John, Sue and Mary are typical. Say why / why not.**

4 Adverbs of frequency

4.1 **Die folgenden Wörter nennt man** *adverbs of frequency* (Adverbien der Häufigkeit):

always never normally
occasionally often rarely
sometimes usually

Ordnen Sie die *adverbs of frequency* **auf dieser Skala ein:**

100 %

0 %

always
usually / ______
______
______
______ / ______
never
______

4.2 **Talk about your eating habits. How often do you do these things?**

1. I [?] drink five or six cups of coffee a day.
2. I [?] eat breakfast in the morning.
3. I [?] have breakfast in bed.
4. I [?] have lunch at the canteen.
5. I [?] eat a hot meal in the evening.
6. I [?] have a cup of coffee after supper.
7. I am [?] at home for supper.
8. At my house, supper is [?] after 6 o'clock.

How romantic! Breakfast in bed!

4.3 **Sehen Sie sich die Sätze in Abschnitt 4.2 noch einmal an. Wo stehen die** *adverbs of frequency?*

Ergänzen Sie: *Adverbs of frequency* stehen meist __________ dem Verb. Ausnahme: das Verb __________ .

4.4 **Talk about breakfast at your house. How often do people in your family eat or drink these things? Use** always, often, sometimes, never **etc.**

My mother always has tea with lemon. She never drinks tea with milk.

5 Eating habits in your class

5.1 Bereiten Sie einen kurzen Artikel über die Eßgewohnheiten in Ihrem Kurs vor. Beantworten Sie nacheinander diese Fragen, und notieren Sie die Antworten der anderen Kursteilnehmer.

What do you normally have for breakfast?
Which is your main meal – breakfast, lunch or supper?
What snacks do you eat between meals?

	breakfast	main meal	snacks
1.			
2.			

5.2 Werten Sie Ihre Notizen aus, und schreiben Sie den Artikel.

Eating habits in my class
... % of students have ...

6 Learning to learn: do-it-yourself English (jumbled sentences)

6.1 Erstellen Sie eigene Übungen, indem Sie Sätze abschreiben und dabei die Wörter durcheinander mischen. Die folgenden Sätze z.B. stammen aus dieser Unit. Können Sie sie wieder richtig ordnen?

What / breakfast / you / do / for / have / normally?
Most / traditional / in / breakfast / have / a / people / Britain / English / never

6.2 Wählen Sie Sätze aus dem Buch oder aus Ihren selbst verfaßten Texten. Geben Sie Ihre Sätze einer anderen Person im Kurs zum Neuordnen. Versuchen Sie selbst nach einigen Tagen, Ihre Sätze wieder neu zu ordnen.

7 Meals in Britain

Read the text and listen to the tape. Then talk about meals in Germany.

The traditional meals are breakfast in the morning, lunch at midday and supper in the evening. Dinner is the main meal of the day. People eat dinner at midday or in the evening. During the working week people usually have dinner in the evening. On Sundays dinner is normally between 12 and 1 pm.

Afternoon tea
Many families still have a traditional afternoon tea on Saturdays or Sundays between 4.30 and 5.30. Afternoon tea always starts with thin, crustless sandwiches (cucumber or watercress). Then follow scones with raspberry or strawberry jam and clotted cream. It ends with various cakes and pastries.

High tea
High tea is an evening meal. It is afternoon tea plus ham or cheese and a salad (lettuce, tomato, cucumber). It is very popular in the north of England and in Scotland.

8 Pronunciation

8.1 The sounds [əʊ] and [aʊ]: Write out the words, eg: [nəʊ] no or [naʊ] now. Then listen and check.

[gəʊ] _______ [haʊ] _______ [həʊm] _______ [haʊs] _______ [fəʊn] _______ [taʊn] _______

8.2 **The sound [ə]: Write out the words with the sound [ə]. Then listen to the tape and check.**

[ə] lot [ə]f wom[ə]n smoke cig[ə]rettes.
My broth[ə]r [ə]nd sist[ə] sleep fr[ə]m ten t[ə] elev[ə]n in th[ə] morning.

8.3 **The sound [ŋ]: Find three more words with [ŋ] as in so<u>ng</u> [sɔŋ] or tha<u>n</u>k [θæŋk].**

9 This takes the cake!

Match the English idioms with the German equivalents.

- a Das ist der Gipfel!
- b Es ist kinderleicht.
- c Man kann nicht alles haben.
- d Das ist nicht mein Bier.
- e Ein Sturm im Wasserglas.
- f Das ist eine andere Sache.
- g Nicht für alles Geld der Welt.
- h Weggehen wie warme Semmeln.

1. ☐ That's not my cup of tea.

2. ☐ A storm in a teacup.

3. ☐ That's another cup of tea.

4. ☐ To sell like hot cakes.

5. ☐ This takes the cake!

6. ☐ It's a piece of cake.

7. ☐ Not for all the tea in China.

8. ☐ To have one's cake and eat it.

10 A song by Herman's Hermits

10.1 Listen to the song. Why is there no milk today?

No milk today
My love has gone away
The bottle stands forlorn
A symbol of the dawn

No milk today
It seems a common sight
But people passing by
Don't know the reason why

How could they know
Just what this message means
The end of my hopes
The end of all my dreams

How could they know
A palace there had been
Behind the door
Where my love reigned as queen

No milk today
It wasn't always so
The company was gay
We turned night into day

But all that's left is a place dark and lonely
A terraced house in a mean street back of town
Becomes a shrine when I think of you only
Just two-up two-down

No milk today
It wasn't always so
The company was gay
We turned night into day

As music played
The faster did we dance
We felt it both at once
The start of our romance

VOCABULARY 1 no kein, keine; 2 has gone away ist weggegangen; 3 to stand forlorn verloren (da)stehen; 4 dawn Morgengrauen; 6 to seem scheinen; a common sight ein gewöhnlicher Anblick; 7 people passing by vorübergehende Leute; 8 reason Grund; 9 could könnte(n); 10 just gerade; message Nachricht; 11 hope Hoffnung; 14 a palace there had been ein Palast war da gewesen; 16 reigned as queen als Königin herrschte; 18 was war; 19 the company was gay *hier:* die Gesellschaft war fröhlich; 20 turned … into verwandelten ... zu; 21 all that's left alles, was übrig ist; a place dark and lonely ein Ort dunkel und einsam; 22 a mean street back of town eine armselige Straße hinten in der Stadt; 23 shrine Schrein; 24 two-up two-down (kleines Reihenhäuschen mit) zwei Zimmer(n) oben, zwei Zimmer(n) unten; 29 as als; played spielte; 30 the faster did we dance umso schneller tanzten wir; 31 we felt it both at once wir fühlten es beide sofort/gleichzeitig; 32 romance Liebe(sgeschichte)

10.2 **The milkman is part of British life. He delivers bottled milk to people's houses every day. He usually comes early in the morning so that people have fresh milk for breakfast. People normally pay for the milk each week.**

Option 3: AFTERNOON TEA

.... *Teekarte aus dem Ritz-Hotel in London*
.... Recipes for afternoon tea: sandwiches and scones

1 Afternoon tea at the Ritz

The Ritz Hotel in London is a popular place for afternoon tea.
It is served at 3.30 pm every day.

Look at this menu for afternoon tea. What would you like to try?

VOCABULARY
served serviert
selection Auswahl
consisting of bestehend aus
smoked salmon geräucherter Lachs
anchovy Sardelle
mustard Senf
cress Kresse
smoked turkey geräucherte Pute
sweet süß
cottage cheese Hüttenkäse
hazelnut Haselnuß
freshly baked frisch gebacken
preserve Konfitüre
choice Auswahl
cream cake Sahne-/Cremetörtchen
camomile tea Kamillentee
blend Mischung
to indulge in sich gönnen
champagne Sekt
to enhance verschönern
to include einschließen
service charge Bedienung
Value Added Tax Mehrwertsteuer

RITZ
AFTERNOON
TEA

Served at 3.30 pm

A selection of sandwiches consisting of:
Smoked salmon
Cucumber and anchovy
Egg mayonnaise with mustard and cress
Smoked turkey and sweet mustard
Cottage cheese with carrot and hazelnuts

Freshly baked scones
with strawberry preserve and clotted cream

A choice of pastries and fresh cream cakes

Indian, China, Earl Grey,
Lapsang, Souchong or Camomile tea
Ritz blend filter coffee
£17.50

Why not indulge in a glass of Ritz Champagne
to enhance your afternoon tea
Glass £6.95 Half bottle £17.00 Bottle £34.00

Prices include service charge and Value Added Tax

2 Recipes for afternoon tea: sandwiches and scones

If you want to have a traditional British afternoon tea, try these recipes.

2.1 Watercress sandwiches

VOCABULARY rye bread Roggenbrot; salty salzig

2.2 Cucumber sandwiches

VOCABULARY vinegar Essig

2.3 Scones

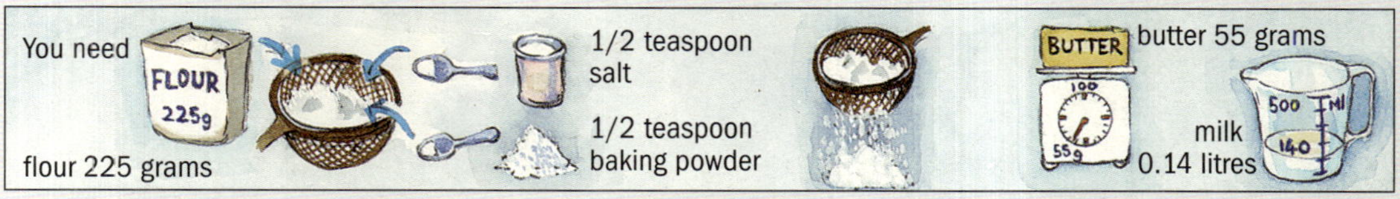

VOCABULARY flour Mehl; teaspoon Teelöffel; baking powder Backpulver; baking sheet Backblech

Serve the scones with clotted cream or butter and strawberry jam. If you cannot find clotted cream, use "crème double".

UNIT 9: LET'S HAVE A PARTY

.... *Mengenangaben:* containers and units
.... *nachfragen, was in welcher Menge für eine Party benötigt wird*
.... how much / how many
.... much / many / a lot of
.... *einen englischen Abend planen und durchführen*

1 Let's have a party

1.1 Listen to the song.

Some people like to rock
Some people like to roll
But moving and grooving
Is not going to satisfy my soul
Let's have a party
We'll send him to the store
Let's buy some more
Let's have a party tonight …

VOCABULARY moving and grooving sich bewegen und sich mitreißen lassen; is not going to wird nicht; to satisfy zufriedenstellen; soul Seele; him ihn

1.2 John and Mary want to have a big party on Saturday. John asks Mary what they need from the supermarket and how much of everything he should get. Read their conversation and listen. Then complete John's shopping list.

John: What do we need from the supermarket?
Mary: Well, first I want to make some sandwiches. So I need a loaf of bread, half a pound of butter, a tin of anchovies, 10 slices of cheese, 12 slices of ham. … Are there many eggs left?
John: No, there aren't. I'll get a dozen eggs. Is that enough?
Mary: Yes, it is.
John: What about tea? Is there much tea left?

Mary: Oh no, there isn't. Get one or two packets of tea and two jars of orange marmalade and also a carton of milk and two cartons of cream … and four or five packets of crisps and a box of chocolates. I also want to serve a salad. There aren't many tomatoes left. But I'll get the vegetables at the market tomorrow morning.
John: What about drinks? How much wine do we need?
Mary: Let's see … How many people are there?
John: About 20, I think.
Mary: That's a lot of people. I think we'll need at least 7 bottles of wine. We don't need to buy much mineral water because there are enough bottles of Highland Spring left.
John: What about orange juice? Is there much orange juice left?
Mary: Yes, there is. But we need some champagne, I think. A lot of people like a glass of champagne in the evening. How many bottles do we need?
John: There's a lot of champagne left-over from my birthday party last month. So we can just use that. And I still have 2 bottles of French champagne. But there's no sherry left. …

Shopping list

1 loaf of bread
1 tin of anchovies
12 slices of ham
2 jars of orange marmalade
2 cartons of cream
4 or 5 packets of crisps
1 box of chocolates

____

____

____

____

____

____

1.3 **Write down the right container or unit.**

1. ______________ *of wine*   2. ______________   3. ______________

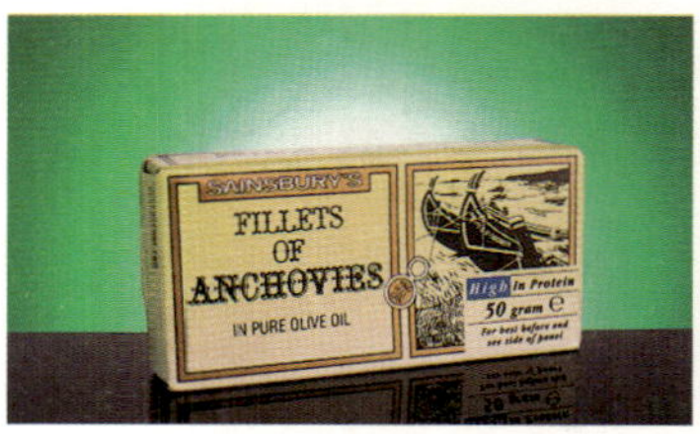

4. ______________   5. ______________   6. ______________ *of chocolates*

7. ______________   8. ______________   9. ______________

2 How much? How many?

2.1 **Wann verwendet man** how much **und wann** how many? **Ergänzen Sie die Regeln. Was bedeuten die Ausdrücke auf deutsch?**

How much wine do we need?

How many bottles do we need?

1. How ____________

(dt.: ____________) verwendet man vor zählbaren Begriffen (Mehrzahlwörter).

2. How ____________

(dt.: ____________) verwendet man vor nicht-zählbaren Begriffen (Einzahlwörter).

2.2 **Make dialogues.**

A: How much wine do we need?
B: We need two bottles of wine.
or: Can you get two bottles of wine, please?

Shopping list

1. wine
2. jam
3. champagne
4. chocolates
5. milk
6. crisps
7. bread
8. eggs
9. cheese
10. tea
11. tomatoes
12. cream
13. mushrooms
14. butter

15. ____________

3 much / many / a lot of

3.1 **Sehen Sie sich die folgenden Beispiele an, und ergänzen Sie dann die Regeln unten für die Verwendung von** much, many **und** a lot of.

We don't need to buy much mineral water.

That's a lot of people.

There's a lot of champagne left-over from my birthday party.

Is there much orange juice left?

There aren't many tomatoes left.

Are there many eggs left?

– In Fragen und verneinten Sätzen verwendet man ____________ oder ____________ .

– In bejahten Sätzen verwendet man ________________ .

3.2 Make dialogues and practise much / many / a lot of. You can use these verbs:

know buy read write have drink eat

A: Do you know many Americans?
B: Yes, I know a lot of Americans.
or: No, I don't know many Americans.

4 An English evening

4.1 Plan a party or an English evening for your class. What do you need for your party? Make a word map.

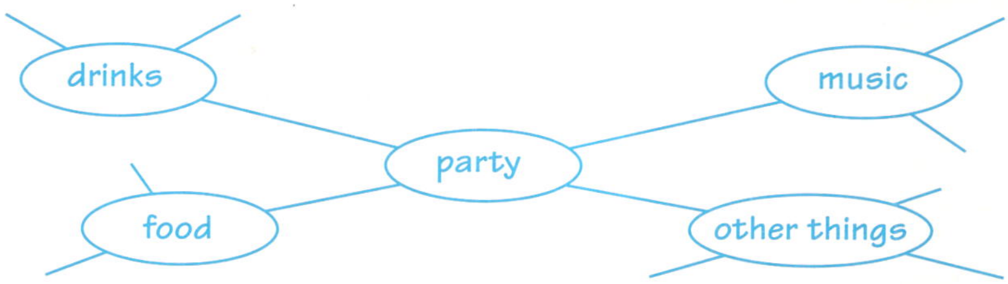

4.2 How much do you need of everything? Make a list. Who can bring what?

What ... you mean NO ONE brought the buns?

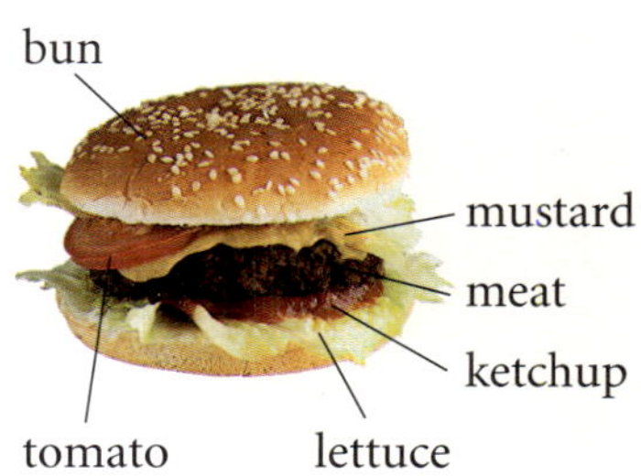

UNIT 10: LIKES AND DISLIKES

.... *Mögen und Nichtmögen ausdrücken*
.... *zustimmen* (So/Nor do I; I do too; I don't either.)
.... *widersprechen* (Do you? I don't; Don't you? I do.)
.... *etwas berichten*
.... *telefonieren*
.... object pronouns (me, you, him, her *etc.*)
.... word order (adverbials of place and time)
.... *Text:* What do they like about Great Britain?
.... *Lerntechnik: zu einem Text ein* word map *anlegen*

1 What do you think of her?

What do you think of the people and cities in the pictures? Do you like them? Talk about the pictures.

A: What do you think of Michelle Pfeiffer?
B: I like her. She's beautiful. … What do you think of the Rolling Stones?
A: I don't mind them. I think they're OK. … Do you like …?

What do you think of …?
Do you like …?

I	like don't like hate love don't mind don't know	him. her. it. them.

I think	he's she's it's they're	OK. boring. interesting. beautiful. handsome. ugly. nice. horrible. funny. entertaining.

2 What kind of films do they like?

2.1 What films do you like? Take notes and report to the class.

westerns

romance films

war films

science fiction

documentaries

horror films

detective films

action films

comedies

2.2 Sarah Ford wants to know what kind of films Jane and Kevin like. Listen and complete the table.

	documentaries	romance films	war films
a) Jane 	likes them		
b) Kevin 			

2.3 Read the dialogues in the Tapescript. What do Kevin and Jane say about the films? Why do they like them? Why don't they like them? Write down two or three sentences about Jane and about Kevin.

Jane says she likes documentaries because they are interesting. She says ...

3 What kind of music do you like?

3.1 What do you think of these types of music?

Ask a partner. Do you like and dislike the same things? Make notes.

A: What do you think of ____________ ?

B: I like | it / them | very much. / a lot.
I love | it. / them.

A: So do I. / I do too. — Do you? I don't.

B: I don't like | it / them | very much. / much. / at all.

A: Nor do I. / I don't either. — Don't you? I do.

3.2 Use your notes and report to the class.

Christiane likes country music and I do too. She doesn't like operas and nor do I. Christiane also likes blues very much, and so do I. She likes techno, but I don't.

3.3 When and where do you listen to music? Do you listen to different types of music at different times of the day? Do you have a favourite piece of music? What is it? What do you think about when you hear it? Tell the other students in the class.

3.4 Write about a piece of music that you like. Read your notes to the class.

One of my favourite pieces of music is L'estate by Vivaldi. I always think about hot summer days in a beautiful garden when I hear it.

I don't have a favourite piece of music, but right now I like Shiny Happy People by R.E.M. When I hear it I want to dance. I don't normally like pop music very much, but Shiny Happy People is a very good song.

4 Vocabulary revision: food and drink

Look again at the vocabulary from Unit 5 (fruit and vegetables) and Units 8 and 9 (food and drink). Say what you like or don't like. Use different expressions.

I like peaches.

I hate onions.

I don't like milk very much.

5 Telephone talk

5.1 Read the text. Then listen. Which dialogue is on the tape?

Robert: Hello. 276 8765.
Lorna: Hello. Could I speak to Sandra, please?

a)

Robert: Yes, of course. Just a moment. I'll get her for you.
Lorna: Thank you.
Robert: Sandra! … Telephone! … It's for you!
Sandra: Hello?
Lorna: Hello, Sandra. This is Lorna. Listen, there is an R.E.M. concert tonight. Would you like to come? I have two free tickets.
Sandra: Oh, do you? I love R.E.M. …

b)

Robert: I'm sorry. She's not in. Can I give her a message?
Lorna: Yes, please. This is Lorna. Can you ask Sandra to call me back this afternoon? She has my number.
Robert: Yes, of course.
Lorna: Thank you. Goodbye.
Robert: Goodbye.

5.2 On the telephone: fill in the correct expressions.

Wie meldet sich Robert am Telefon? ____________________

Wie verlangt Lorna Sandra? ____________________

Wie drückt Robert aus, daß er Lorna holen wird? ____________________

Wie drückt man „Hier ist (+ Name)" auf englisch aus? ____________________

Was sagen Robert und Lorna anstelle von „Auf Wiederhören"? ____________________

5.3 Make telephone calls. You can use these names and numbers. Reverse roles.

The Queen	0171 132 5433	Paul McCartney	0141 331 5798
Lady Diana	0171 347 6653	Anthony Hopkins	01608 612518
Margaret Thatcher	01844 348876	The Prime Minister	0171 684 9977

6 Word order

6.1 Listen to the messages on Robert and Sandra King's answering machine. Underline the wrong parts in the following texts. Then listen again and write the correct messages.

1. Hello, Robert. This is Richard. I can't meet you for lunch tomorrow. I'll call you at home this evening. Bye.
2. Hi, it's Sally! Lorna, I'll call you back later. It's about the party at Mary's office on Friday.
3. This is Ann Landers calling for Lorna. Please call me at my sister's house this afternoon. The number is 682 4556.
4. This is Fred Miller of Worldwide Travel. Mr King, can you pick up your travel documents from our office after 8 o'clock tonight? If not, please call us.

6.2 In welcher Reihenfolge stehen im Englischen Ergänzungen des Ortes und der Zeit? Und im Deutschen?

Englisch: ________________ vor ________________

Deutsch: ________________ vor ________________

6.3 Translate these sentences.

1. Ruf mich vor 6 Uhr im Büro an.
2. Es geht um die Party am Wochenende bei Mike zu Hause.
3. Ich kann dich am Samstag nicht auf dem Markt treffen.
4. Bitte holen Sie Ihre Eintrittskarten heute nachmittag in unserem Büro ab.

7 Object pronouns

7.1 Wörter wie me, him, her **etc., die anstelle eines Objekts stehen, nennt man** *object pronouns.* **Unterstreichen Sie alle** *object pronouns* **in diesem Cartoon.**

7.2 **Tragen Sie die *object pronouns* in die Tabelle ein.**

subject pronouns	I	you	he	she	it	we	they
object pronouns	______	______	______	______	______	______	______

7.3 **Fill in the gaps.**

1. I'm sorry I can't see ______ tomorrow, Tom. But I can call ______ .
2. Anne's phone number? Sorry, I don't have ______ .
3. Hotel California. Can I help ______?
4. Billy, Charly and I want to go to the cinema tonight. Do you want to come with ______ ?

5. My new job? It's wonderful. I love ______ .
6. Anne and Andrew! … Telephone! … It's for ______ !

7. Spanish? I can understand ______ , but I don't speak ______ .
8. Our children? Oh, they both live in London now. They don't often visit ______ , so we sometimes visit ______ at the weekend.
9. No, I don't know Susan. But I would like to meet ______ . Can you give ______ my number when you see ______ next week?
10. My son? He lives in Hawaii. He writes ______ a letter every month. I see ______ every winter.

8 Pronunciation

8.1 **Listen to the following sentences and underline the sound [ɒ] as in sh<u>o</u>p.**

What a horrible opera. The doctor wants to take a walk. I want to go to the office tomorrow.

8.2 **Write out the words with the sound [ɔː] as in <u>all</u>. Then listen to the tape.**

[ɔː]ll l[ɔː]yers t[ɔː]k. C[ɔː]ll y[ɔː] d[ɔː]ter in [ɔː]stria.

8.3 **[uː] or [ʊ]? Listen and mark long [uː] as in f<u>oo</u>d or short [ʊ] as in good.**

A good book about football. Who has two spoons? Look at the beautiful woman in the blue room. Do you eat fruit? He reads the newspaper in the afternoon.

8.4 **Write out these words with the sound [ɔɪ]: [bɔɪfrend] __________ and [tɔɪlət] __________ .**

9 What do they like about Britain?

9.1 Four foreigners talk about Britain. They are from Austria, France, Germany and the United States. Listen and read. Then match the pictures with the statements and say where each person is from.

What do you like about Britain?

1. ☐

2. ☐

3. ☐

4. ☐

a

What I like about Britain? Well, British pubs are very nice, you know, with the atmosphere and the interior decoration. You go to a pub in Britain and it's like you're in somebody's living room! And I love a glass of real British ale. I like the shorter meal times in Britain too. Here people don't spend hours at the table. You have more time to do what you want, for example, on Sunday afternoon you can watch football on television. People can't do that in my country because for many families Sunday dinner is from one to four.

I think he is from ______________________.

b

I love the British countryside, the little villages, the old country homes with their beautiful English gardens. A lot of houses have very nice lawns too and in June you can see beautiful rose gardens all over Britain. I like the people too. British people are very friendly. New neighbours invite you for tea and offer to help you with your shopping, your new house, the garden. I come from a big city where many people don't know their neighbours. I also like British drivers. They are very disciplined. Driving is very safe in Britain.

She is from ______________________.

c

I like Britain because life is so relaxed there. For many British people work is not so important. They like their holidays, their animals, their homes and gardens. Holidays in Britain are longer too and I like that because I have more time for my family. Life is very safe in Britain, even in London. That's important for me because I have two small children. And London is a very clean city too. I love all the great historical places all over Britain and the old traditions. We don't have a long history in my country. But many people in Britain are cold and not very open. It takes a long time to make friends. And the shops close too early.

This woman comes from ______________.

d

Believe it or not, I like the weather. You can have sun, wind, rain, snow and fog – all in one day! It's never boring. Britain has so many beautiful coastlines, for example in Wales, Cornwall, Scotland … My country doesn't have a coastline and I love the sea. I like London because there are so many things to do there. There are so many theatres, museums, cinemas, pubs, discos, music clubs where you can hear live music. And then there's all those ethnic restaurants in London too: Indian, Pakistani, Caribbean, African, French, Italian. London has a great ethnic mix. It's a very cosmopolitan city. I think British people are very tolerant.

I believe this man is from ______________.

9.2 **Stellen Sie zu dem Thema** Britain **ein** word map **her. Verwenden Sie möglichst viele der neuen Wörter und Ausdrücke.**

Versuchen Sie dann, mit Hilfe Ihres word map **die Eindrücke der vier Personen von Großbritannien wiederzugeben.**

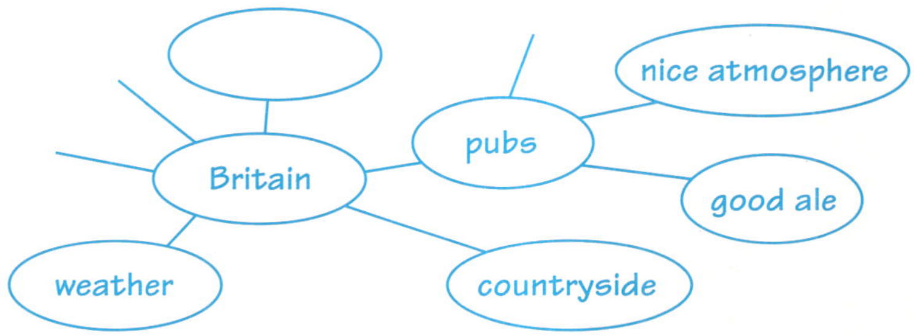

Britain has … British people are … In London there are … In Britain you can … etc.

9.3 **Versetzen Sie sich in die Rolle eines in Deutschland lebenden Amerikaners oder Briten. Was würde er (oder sie) wohl zu den folgenden Bereichen sagen?**

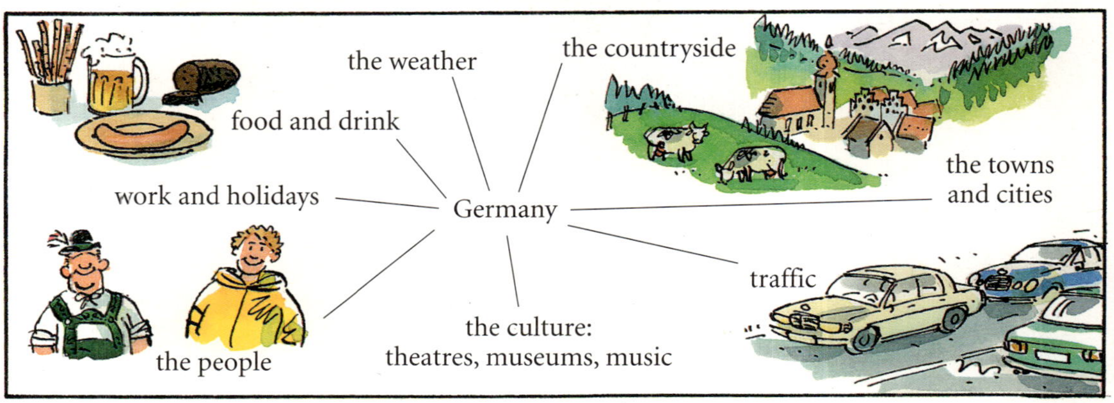

Machen Sie Notizen, und erstellen Sie dann einen kurzen Text. Lesen Sie ihn vor.

An English woman in Germany
She likes Germany because …

An Englishman in Germany
He thinks …

An American in Germany
He (She) loves …
He (She) doesn't like …

UNIT 11: SUGGESTIONS

.... *sich begrüßen und verabschieden*
.... *sich verabreden*
.... *einen Vorschlag machen*
.... *einen Vorschlag annehmen oder ablehnen*
.... *einen Gegenvorschlag machen*
.... *Bedauern und Begeisterung ausdrücken*

1 Would you like to come with me?

1.1 Sandra and Lorna meet in the street. Listen to their conversation. Then answer the questions.

1. Where does Sandra work?
2. What does she do?
3. What does she think of her job?
4. What does Lorna want to do tonight?
5. When and where will Lorna and Sandra meet?

2 Arranging to meet: useful phrases

2.1 Listen again. What do Lorna and Sandra actually say? Tick the right box or boxes.

1. Sandra begrüßt Lorna.

☐ Good morning, Lorna.
☐ Hello there, Lorna.

2. Lorna begrüßt Sandra und fragt nach ihrem Befinden.

☐ Oh, hello Sandra.
☐ Hi Sandra. Nice to see you.
☐ How are you?

3. Sandra geht es gut.

☐ Oh, I'm great!
☐ I'm fine, thank you.

4. Sie ist begeistert von ihrem Job.

☐ I like my new job very much.
☐ I have this wonderful new job.
☐ I love it!

5. Lorna reagiert auf Sandras Begeisterung.

☐ Oh really? That's great.
☐ Oh, that's wonderful. I'm so happy for you!

6. Sandra fragt nach Lornas Befinden.

☐ Well, how about you, Lorna? How are you these days?
☐ Well, how are things with you, Lorna?

7. Lorna geht es gut.

☐ Not bad, thank you.
☐ Oh, just fine, thanks.

8. Sie macht Sandra einen Vorschlag.

☐ Listen … I have an idea.
☐ Let's go to the cinema tonight.
☐ Hugh Grant's new film is on at the Odeon cinema tonight. I'd like to see it. Would you like to come with me?

9. Sandra nimmt den Vorschlag an.

☐ Oh great! I love Hugh Grant!
☐ That sounds nice. Yes, I'd love to come.

10. Lorna schlägt einen Treffpunkt vor.

☐ Let's have a drink first. We can meet at the pub next to the cinema.
☐ Why don't we meet at the pub next to the cinema? We could have a drink first.

11. Sandra ist einverstanden und fragt wann.

☐ Okay. When?
☐ Yes, fine. What time?

12. Lorna schlägt einen Zeitpunkt vor.

☐ We could meet at 7.30.
☐ Is 7.30 all right?
☐ The film starts at 8.30.

13. Sandra ist einverstanden und verabschiedet sich.

☐ Right. I'll see you tonight. Bye, Lorna.
☐ Okay. See you later. Bye, Lorna.

2.2 **Rekonstruieren Sie den Dialog. Verwenden Sie die Äußerungen, die Sie unter 2.1 angekreuzt haben. Versuchen Sie, die fehlenden Teile aus dem Gedächtnis zu ergänzen. Hören Sie dann nochmal den Dialog.**

3 What's the matter with Sandra?

In the dialogue in section 2 Sandra feels great and she loves her job. The following dialogue is another version of the same situation. Read the dialogue and listen to the tape. Which parts are new?

a)
Sandra: Hello there, Lorna.
Lorna: Hi Sandra. Nice to see you. How are you?

b)
Sandra: Oh, I'm not too well, I'm afraid.
Lorna: I'm sorry to hear that. What's the matter with you?
Sandra: Oh well, I have this new job at the Hotel International and I don't like it very much.
Lorna: Oh really? What do you do there?
Sandra: I'm a switchboard operator. I answer the telephone all day. … It's so boring. Well, how about you, Lorna? How are you these days?

c)
Lorna: Oh, just fine, thanks. Listen … I have an idea. Hugh Grant's new film is on at the Odeon cinema tonight. I'd like to see it. Would you like to come with me?

d)
Sandra: I'm sorry, I can't. I work evenings this week.
Lorna: That's too bad.
Sandra: But I could call you next week when I have some time. We could go for a drink or something.
Lorna: Yes, that's a good idea. Well then, I'll talk to you next week.
Sandra: Okay. Have a nice weekend.
Lorna: Thank you. Same to you.

4 Saying the right thing: useful phrases

4.1 How do you respond in these situations? Check again the dialogues in sections 2 and 3, if necessary.

1. Jemand fragt Sie nach Ihrem Befinden. — Ihnen geht es schlecht.

2. Jemand teilt Ihnen etwas Negatives mit. — Sie drücken Ihr Bedauern auf die Mitteilung aus.

   I don't like my job. — I'm sorry ______

   I work evenings. — That's ______

3. Jemand macht einen Vorschlag. — Sie nehmen den Vorschlag an.

   Let's have a drink first. — ______

   Sie lehnen den Vorschlag ab, bedauern und begründen dies und machen einen Gegenvorschlag.

   Would you like to come to the cinema with me? — I'm sorry, ______

   ______

4. Jemand wünscht Ihnen ein schönes Wochenende. — Sie geben den Wunsch zurück.

   Have a nice weekend. — Thank you. ______

4.2 Stellen Sie sich vor, Sie treffen einen englischen Freund oder eine Freundin zufällig auf der Straße. Machen Sie sich Stichpunkte, wie ein Gespräch mit ihm oder ihr ablaufen könnte. Verwenden Sie möglichst viele der Formulierungen aus Abschnitt 2.1 und 4.1. Achten Sie darauf, daß Sie nur über Dinge sprechen, die Sie auf englisch auch ausdrücken können. Spielen Sie dann anhand Ihrer Notizen das Gespräch auf englisch durch, und tragen Sie es der Gruppe vor.

Hello there!

5 Suggestions

5.1 Sandra doesn't like her job. What do you think she could do about it? Do you have a suggestion?

Make some suggestions. Collect your ideas on the blackboard. Ask your teacher if you need new words.

She can ______________________

She could ______________________

Why doesn't she ______________________

5.2 Imagine that you got a letter from Sandra. Answer her letter. Tell her what she could do about her job. Talk about yourself too. You could start like this:

Dear Sandra,
Thank you for your letter.
I am sorry that you don't like your job.
I have some suggestions ...
You want to know how I am. Well, I am ...

6 Let's get together to study English ...

Verabreden Sie sich mit anderen aus dem Kurs zum Englischlernen. Legen Sie Ort und Zeit fest. Tips, wie Sie zu Hause mit anderen zusammen lernen können, finden Sie in *Option* 4.

7 Pronunciation

7.1 You find these sounds before the letter r:

[ɜː] as in sir [ɪə] as in here [eə] as in there [ʊə] as in cure [ɔː] as in more

In each list one word is wrong. Cross it out and write it in the right list. Then listen to the tape and repeat the words.

1. [ɜː] firm learn dear purse work ______
2. [ɪə] near we're hear first ______
3. [eə] where their pair pear during ______
4. [ʊə] you're tourist four ______
5. [ɔː] door morning your north war wear ______

7.2 Write out the following sentences. Then listen to the tape and check.

1. ðə wʊmən wɪð ðə pɜːpl pɜːs wɜːks ən θhɜːzdeɪ
2. wɪə hɪə dɪə
3. ðeər‿ɑː nəʊ peəz ən ðə tʃeəz
4. jʊər‿ə tʊərɪst
5. weər‿ɪz jʊə dɒg ɪn ðə mɔːnɪŋ?

Option 4: STUDYING TOGETHER

.... *Übungen zum gemeinsamen Englischlernen*
.... *Lerntechniken zur Wiederholung von Vokabeln und zum Einüben von Alltagsdialogen*

1 Verbs, verbs, verbs

1.1 **Vor Unit 12 empfiehlt es sich, die wichtigsten Verben zu wiederholen.**

a) Schreiben Sie Verben und Ausdrücke mit Verben auf, die eine konkrete Tätigkeit beschreiben:

ride a bicycle   sleep   make a cake   read

b) Stellen Sie diese Tätigkeiten pantomimisch dar, oder fertigen Sie Zeichnungen davon an. Die anderen müssen raten.

1.2 **Fassen Sie die Tätigkeiten zu sinnvollen Paaren zusammen.**

a) gegensätzliche oder sich ergänzende Tätigkeiten: read – write   eat – drink   sleep – wake up

b) zeitliche Abläufe:

Lesen Sie dann jeweils den ersten Teil Ihrer Kombinationen vor. Die anderen versuchen, den zweiten Teil zu erraten. Gibt es Kombinationen, die niemand erraten hat?

2 Dialogues

Wählen Sie einen Dialog von der Kassette. Jeder übernimmt eine Rolle. Hören Sie den Dialog, und versuchen Sie gleichzeitig, zu Ihrer Rolle Stichpunkte zu machen. Versuchen Sie dann, anhand Ihrer Notizen das gesamte Gespräch wieder aufzubauen.

Die Notizen für ein Gespräch aus der letzten Unit würden zum Beispiel so aussehen:

Sandra: hello
Lorna: –
Sandra: great / wonderful job
Lorna: –
Sandra: switchboard operator / interesting / talk to people / French and Spanish / you?

Sandra: –
Lorna: nice ... / how?
Sandra: –
Lorna: ? / great / what?
Sandra: –

Weitere Vorschläge, wie Sie Dialoge zu zweit einüben können, finden Sie im Lernerhandbuch.

3 Word chains

Bilden Sie Wortketten: word dream mother radio

Jedes Wort darf nur einmal vorkommen.

4 Odd one out

4.1 Bilden Sie Wortreihen, bei denen ein Wort nicht zu den anderen paßt:

1. sofa chair cucumber table
2. red small yellow blue
3. interesting live write swim

Lesen Sie dann nacheinander Ihre Wortreihen vor.
Die anderen nennen die Wörter, die nicht dazugehören, und schreiben sie auf.

4.2 Schreiben Sie eine Geschichte, in der alle Wörter vorkommen, die oben nicht in die Wortreihen paßten. Versuchen Sie, Ihre Geschichte so kurz wie möglich zu halten. Lesen Sie Ihre Geschichte vor.

5 What is it?

5.1 Schreiben Sie drei beliebige Begriffe auf drei kleine Zettel (z.B. school oder eat), und fügen Sie jeweils drei englische Wörter hinzu, die Sie spontan mit dem Begriff assoziieren:

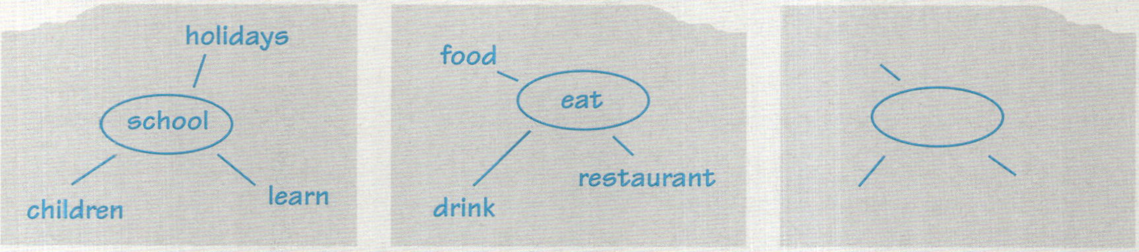

5.2 Tauschen Sie die Zettel aus. Versuchen Sie, die einzelnen Begriffe auf englisch zu beschreiben, ohne die drei Wörter zu verwenden. Die anderen müssen den Begriff erraten.

Teachers work there.

You have a sandwich on your plate. What do you do with it?

UNIT 12: CHILDHOOD MEMORIES

.... *über Vergangenes sprechen*
.... *das* past simple *von* to be *(Aussageform, Verneinung, Frage)*
.... *das* past simple *der regelmäßigen und unregelmäßigen Verben (Aussageform)*
.... *Techniken zum Lernen der unregelmäßigen Verben*
.... *Text:* The little girl and the wolf (James Thurber)

1 My first memory

1.1 Sarah Ford asks Mrs Blake and Jack Sands about their first memories. Listen and read.

a)

Sarah Ford: Mrs Blake, what is your first memory?

Mrs Blake: I can't remember much. My parents were from London, but we were in Scotland during the war.

Sarah Ford: How old were you?

Mrs Blake: I was five or six. I remember the village. It was very different then. There was no school and there wasn't much traffic then. There weren't many people in the village during the war, only some farmers and their families. They were very nice to us. My little brother was very happy there.

A Scottish village in the 1940s.

Now look at these questions and underline the correct answer.

1. Were Mrs Blake's parents from London?	Yes, they were. / No, they weren't.
2. Was Mrs Blake in London during the war?	Yes, she was. / No, she wasn't.
3. Was there a school in the village?	Yes, there was. / No, there wasn't.
4. Were there many people in the village?	Yes, there were. / No, there weren't.
5. Was Mrs Blake's brother unhappy there?	Yes, he was. / No, he wasn't.

b)

Sarah Ford: What is your first memory, Jack?

Jack Sands: Oh gosh. That's a difficult question. What is the first thing I can remember? Yes. It was when I was three. My brother was four. We were in our room. It was at night. Our parents weren't at home. The window was open. ... Suddenly there was a cat in the window. It was black with yellow eyes. It wasn't afraid, but we were!

Answer the questions.

1. How old were Jack and his brother?
2. Where were their parents?
3. What time of day was it?
4. What colour was the cat?
5. Who was afraid?

1.2 **Sarah also asks Lee Benson. Listen and read. Then ask questions about the dialogue.**

Sarah Ford: What's your first memory?
Lee Benson: My first memory? That was a long time ago! I remember my first day at school. I was five years old. The classroom was very big and there were lots of other pupils. The blackboard wasn't black, it was green. My teacher was very nice. What was her name? I think it was Mrs Spender ... No, that's not right ... Mrs Spencer was her name. She was American.

1.3 **Make a short summary of Mrs Blake's or Jack Sand's or Lee Benson's first memory. Do not look at the texts again, if possible.**

2 The past simple of *to be*

2.1 **Fill in the** *past simple* **forms of the verb** to be.

Positive statements

I / He / She / It ________ in Scotland.

We / You / They ________ five years old.

There ________ a cinema.

There ________ a lot of shops.

Negatives

It ________ (= was not) afraid.

They ________ (= were not) at home.

Questions

________ she in London?

How old ________ you?

________ there many people in the village?

2.2 **Fill in** was, were, wasn't **or** weren't.

Our holiday this year ________ wonderful. We ________ in Brighton. The weather ________ beautiful for September. Our hotel ________ expensive (only £300 for two weeks) and the food ________ good too.

My parents ________ in Benicante in August. They ________ happy there at all. Their hotel ________ expensive and the food ________ very good. There ________ too many English tourists.

3 How was your town different before?

Talk about your town one year ago, five years ago and ten years ago.

One year ago, there was a cinema in Königstraße.
Five years ago, there was no swimming-pool.
Ten years ago, there weren't many tourists here.
Ten years ago, there were a lot of small shops in the centre of the town.

4 Childhood stories and fairy tales

4.1 Listen and read. Then match the characters with the stories on page 101.

a I lived near Nottingham in a forest. I had a lot of friends. My best friend was Little John. We took things from rich people and gave them to poor people. The Sheriff of Nottingham hated us. He tried to find us in the forest, but he couldn't.

b My mother and I were hungry. We needed food, but we had no money. My mother wanted to sell an old lamp and started to clean it. Suddenly a genie came out. He said he was the slave of the owner of the lamp. He brought us food on silver dishes. We sold the empty dishes and got a lot of money for them. One day I saw the sultan's daughter and fell in love with her. I asked the genie to make me a rich man. He did a lot of other things for me too. In the end I married the sultan's daughter and became a king.

c My mother made a cake and told me to take it to my grandmother. When I arrived at her house I found somebody else in her bed. The person had very big eyes, ears, nose and teeth – it was a wolf! The wolf ate me but later some men came and opened up the wolf and took me out.

d I lived in a castle with my stepmother. She was horrible. I ran away and stayed with seven dwarfs. But my stepmother found me. She wanted to kill me because I was beautiful. She gave me a poisoned apple and I ate it. She thought I was dead, but I wasn't. I slept for a long time. When I woke up, I saw a prince. The prince said that he loved me and we got married. I felt very happy.

e I lived with my two ugly stepsisters and my stepmother. They were horrible. They said I couldn't go to the ball at the prince's palace. A fairy gave me a wonderful dress and I went to the ball. I met the prince and danced with him. I stayed until midnight. When I wanted to leave, I dropped a glass shoe. The prince found it and sent out his men to find the girl with the other glass shoe. When the prince's men came to our house, my stepsisters tried to put on the glass shoe, but it was too small for them. When I tried on the shoe, the prince's men knew that I was the right girl. The prince asked me to become his wife and we had a big wedding.

4.2 **Versuchen Sie, so viele der neuen Vokabeln und Ausdrücke aus 4.1 wie möglich zu einem** word map **um die Begriffe** rich – poor – good – bad **herum zusammenzustellen.**

5 The past simple: regular and irregular verbs

5.1 Read the texts in section 4.1 again and underline all forms of the *past simple*. Try to find the infinitives. Make a list in your exercise book. Compare your list with a neighbour.

lived – to live
had – to have

5.2 Now complete the table and fill in the *past simple* forms (I, you, he, she, it, we, they) of the following regular and irregular verbs.

Regular verbs

to arrive	______	to hate	______	to marry	______
to ask	______	to need	______	to try	______
to dance	______	to start	______		
to live	______	to want	______	to drop	______
to love	______				
to open	______				
to stay	______				

Irregular verbs

to be	______	to get	______	to see	______
to become	______	to give	______	to sell	______
to bring	______	to go	______	to send	______
to come	______	to have	______	to sleep	______
to do	______	to know	______	to take	______
to eat	______	to make	______	to tell	______
to fall	______	to meet	______	to think	______
to feel	______	to run	______	to wake up	______
to find	______	to say	______	can	______

5.3 Ergänzen Sie die Regeln.

1. Die *past-simple*-Form der regelmäßigen Verben bildet man durch Anhängen von ______ .
2. Bei der Schreibung der regelmäßigen *past-simple*-Formen muß man folgendes beachten: Endet ein Verb

– auf -e (z.B. like), ______

– auf Konsonant + y (z.B. try), ______

– auf einen Konsonanten nach einem kurzen, betonten Vokal: (z.B. stop), ______

3. Die *past-simple*-Formen sind in allen Personen (I, you, he, she, it, we, they) gleich.

Die einzige Ausnahme ist das Verb ______ .

6 Regular verbs

Listen to the *past simple* forms of the *regular verbs* on the tape. What's the correct pronunciation of the ending?

	1	2	3	4	5	6	7	8	9	10	11	12	13	14
[t]														
[d]	x													
[ɪd]														

Nach welchen Endbuchstaben spricht man die Endung -ed [ɪd] aus?

7 Learning irregular verbs

Versuchen Sie, die neuen Verbformen mit Hilfe dieser nonsense-Sätze zu lernen.

a) Fill in the days of the week and read this rhyme aloud.

David D Dunday

met Mary on M________________

told Tina a tall tale on ________________

went to Wales on ________________

thought he was thirty on ________________

felt funny on ________________

sold his sofa on ________________

slept until seven on ________________ –

and that was a week

in the life of David D Dunday.

b) Find the "right" ending for each sentence. Then read the sentences aloud.

Amanda **a**te	a **b**utler in **B**irmingham.
Bill **b**ecame	with a **c**ook from **K**ansas.
Bob **b**rought	**a**n apple from **A**labama.
Kevin **c**ame	**f**our **f**ried eggs in the **f**reezer.
Diana **d**id	**B**renda a **b**anana from **B**oston.
Fiona **f**ell	a **g**reat job in **G**reenville.
Fred **f**ound	his **g**irlfriend a **g**rey cat.
Gary **g**ave	the **d**ishes in **D**enver.
Greg **g**ot	asleep in **F**lorida.
Harry **h**ad	a **m**ilkshake in **M**iami.
Nina **kn**ew	**n**othing about **N**ew York.
Mary **m**ade	**T**ed the **t**rue story about **T**om.
Sally **s**aid	that she was the **s**ultan's **s**ecretary.
Susan **s**aw	to **w**ork in **W**ashington.
Tina **t**old	a **h**oliday **h**ome in **H**awaii.
Wendy **w**ent	his **w**onderful **w**ife in **W**isconsin.
Walter **w**oke up	**s**ome **s**now in **S**eattle.

8 A fable by James Thurber

8.1 Look at the pictures before you read the fable. How is it different from the traditional fairy tale?

The Little Girl and the Wolf

One afternoon a big wolf waited in a dark forest for a little girl to come along carrying a basket of food to her grandmother. Finally a little girl did come along and she was carrying a basket of food. "Are you carrying that basket to your grandmother?" asked the wolf. The little girl said yes, she was. So the wolf asked her where her grandmother lived and the little girl told him and he disappeared into the wood.
When the little girl opened the door of her grandmother's house she saw that there was somebody in bed with a nightcap and nightgown on. She had approached no nearer than twenty-five feet from the bed when she saw that it was not her grandmother but the wolf, for even in a nightcap a wolf does not look any more like your grandmother than the Metro-Goldwyn lion looks like Calvin Coolidge. So the little girl took an automatic out of her basket and shot the wolf dead.

Moral: It is not so easy to fool little girls nowadays as it used to be.

8.2 **Answer these questions.**

1. Do you like the fable? What do you think of the moral?
2. The comparison between the Metro-Goldwyn lion and Calvin Coolidge is not up-to-date for today's readers. Can you find two people from public life today and make a funny comparison?

8.3 **Choose another fairy tale. Rewrite it with a surprise ending. Read it to the rest of the class.**

9 Learning with pictures

9.1 **Sehen Sie sich die Bilder unter Abschnitt 8.1 an, und versuchen Sie, die Handlung der Fabel im *past simple* nachzuerzählen.**

9.2 **Hören Sie sich die Geschichten unter Abschnitt 4.1 noch einmal in Ruhe an. Schließen Sie dabei die Augen, und visualisieren Sie die Handlung der einzelnen Geschichten. Versuchen Sie, zu jedem Satz eine bildliche Vorstellung zu entwickeln. Diese können ruhig etwas übertrieben sein.**

Versuchen Sie dann, sich die ganze Geschichte bildlich vorzustellen, und ergänzen Sie den passenden Text aus dem Gedächtnis.

Wenn Sie Spaß am Zeichnen haben, können Sie Ihre bildlichen Vorstellungen auch zu Papier bringen und anhand Ihrer Zeichnungen die Geschichte rekonstruieren.

Tips zum Lernen weiterer unregelmäßiger Verben finden Sie in *Option* 5.

Option 5: VERBS, VERBS, VERBS

.... *Techniken zum Lernen der unregelmäßigen* past-simple-*Formen*
.... *Song:* Yesterday (The Beatles)
.... the past simple: *Frage und Verneinung mit* did (preview)

1 Tips for learning irregular verbs

Die folgende Liste enthält weitere unregelmäßige *past-simple*-Formen von Verben, deren Infinitive Sie bereits aus den Units 1–12 kennen.
Alle anderen Verben, die in Unit 1–12 bis jetzt vorkamen, haben regelmäßige *past-simple*-Formen.

to break	broke	to lie	lay	to spell	spelt
to buy	bought	to mean	meant [ment]	to spend	spent
to choose	chose	to pay	paid	to stand	stood
to drink	drank	to put	put	to swim	swam
to drive	drove	to read	read [red]	to understand	understood
to hear	heard [hɜːd]	to ride	rode	to wear	wore
to learn	learnt	to shoot	shot	to write	wrote
to leave	left	to sing	sang		
to let	let	to speak	spoke		

Da zwischen den einzelnen Verben keinerlei inhaltlicher oder formaler Zusammenhang besteht, fällt es schwer, sie anhand einer Liste zu lernen und sich dann im Bedarfsfall auch noch an die richtige Form zu erinnern. Deshalb müssen Sie versuchen, selbst sinnhafte Zusammenhänge herzustellen, in denen Sie die unregelmäßigen Verben besser lernen und behalten können. Die folgenden Lerntechniken dienen Ihnen dabei als Anregung. Suchen Sie sich das Verfahren aus, das Ihnen persönlich am meisten zusagt.

1.1 **Verbinden Sie die zu lernenden Verbformen mit bestimmten Orten, die Sie gut kennen.**

**a) Stellen Sie sich vor, Sie gehen in Ihrem Wohnort spazieren.
Schreiben Sie so viele Orte wie möglich auf, an denen Sie vorbeikommen:**

cinema   Hilton hotel   market   supermarket   chemist's

b) Verbinden Sie jeden dieser Orte mit einem unregelmäßigen Verb, und bilden Sie Sätze in der Vergangenheit:

Yesterday, Beate and I saw a film at the cinema.
We had a drink at the Hilton hotel.
We bought vegetables at the market.
We went to the supermarket.
We met Sabine at the chemist's.

1.2 Schreiben Sie selbst nonsense-Sätze mit den neuen Formen, die Sie lernen möchten, zum Beispiel so:

Bill bought bread and butter in Birmingham.
Charlie chose cheese in Chester. ...

1.3 Mimen Sie die Vergangenheit. Stellen Sie unregelmäßige Verben, die sich dafür eignen, pantomimisch dar. Die anderen müssen raten und nennen jeweils den Infinitiv und die *past-simple*-Form.

1.4 Lernen Sie in Bildern, und stellen Sie neue Gedankenverbindungen mit den zu lernenden Verbformen her: Sehen Sie sich ein Photo an, und versuchen Sie, die Verben, die Sie lernen wollen, irgendwie damit zu assoziieren.

Nehmen Sie beispielsweise dieses Urlaubsphoto als Ausgangspunkt, und malen Sie sich aus, was sich dort abgespielt haben könnte. Vielleicht können Sie eine kleine Geschichte entwickeln. Übrigens: Je »merk-würdiger« Ihre Geschichte ist, desto besser werden Sie sie behalten.

Stellen Sie sich die weiteren Ereignisse als Bildfolge vor, und versprachlichen Sie die einzelnen Bilder mit den zu lernenden Verben.

Last summer at the Hotel California

Tom Cruise bought me flowers.

We had dinner at a restaurant.

We went to the beach.

1.5 **Lernen Sie mit Musik. Hören Sie sich ein englisches Lied an, das Sie mögen. Denken Sie sich eine Szene aus, die dazu paßt und die sich mit den neuen Verbformen beschreiben läßt.**

Versuchen Sie es einmal mit Yesterday **von den Beatles. Hören Sie das Lied auf der Kassette an.**

Yesterday,
all my troubles seemed so far away,
now it looks as though they're here to stay,
oh, I believe in yesterday.

Suddenly,
I'm not half the man I used to be,
there's a shadow hanging over me,
oh, yesterday came suddenly.

Why she had to go I don't know,
she wouldn't say,
I said something wrong,
now I long for yesterday.

Yesterday,
love was such an easy game to play,
now I need a place to hide away,
oh, I believe in yesterday.

Führen Sie dann die Erinnerungen des Sängers an yesterday **weiter aus: Wie könnte eine Beschreibung des sorgenfreien Lebens, das er** yesterday **genoß, lauten? Entwickeln Sie eine kleine Geschichte, und verwenden Sie möglichst viele der Verbformen, die Sie sich merken wollen.**

Yesterday, all my troubles seemed so far away ... We were happy together. We had ...

2 Test yourself: past simple forms

Can you find all the forms of the past simple in the square?

They begin with the following first letters:

P	A	I	D	E	I	N	V	I	T	E	D	T	H	O	F	E
L	E	T	L	S	A	W	T	H	O	U	G	H	T	P	O	S
A	T	E	L	M	F	E	L	T	O	F	F	E	R	E	D	O
Y	P	M	S	A	I	D	M	S	K	I	F	O	U	N	D	L
E	N	D	E	D	S	P	E	X	P	L	A	I	N	E	D	D
D	H	A	D	E	A	T	T	F	O	S	R	E	A	D	R	M

F OUND	O ______	P ______	S ______
O ______	F ______	A ______	I ______
R ______		S ______	M ______
M ______	T ______	T ______	P ______
S ______	H ______		L ______
	E ______		E ______

3 Preview: How to make questions and negative sentences in the past simple

Erinnern Sie sich, wie man Frage und Verneinung im *present simple* bildet?
Hier ist ein Beispiel aus einem Cartoon:

Im *past simple* werden Frage und Verneinung auf ähnliche Weise gebildet, nämlich mit did und dem *infinitive*.
Ein weiteres Beispiel aus dem gleichen Cartoon:

Was hätte Charlie gesagt, wenn er den Umschlag des Comic-Heftes nicht abgerissen hätte?

No, I ____________ tear the cover off this comic magazine.

In Eurolingua Band 1B erfahren Sie mehr über die Frage und Verneinung im *past simple.*

4 A word box

Use the words in the word box and make questions and negative sentences in the *past simple.*

did	give	New York	yesterday	go
Peter	what	you	television	children
a	to	where	they	eat
buy	letter	watch	when	on
didn't	the	newspaper	send	get up

Examples:
Did Peter watch television yesterday?
Peter didn't read a letter.

5 A cartoon

Look at the Peanuts cartoon below. Match the questions and the pictures.

1. ☐ Why do you do such stupid things?
2. ☐ Why don't I think?
3. ☐ Did you tear the cover off this comic magazine?
4. ☐ Am I really responsible?
5. ☐ Who is responsible?

VOCABULARY stupid dumm; responsible verantwortlich; blockhead Dummkopf; I guess ich glaube; myself mich (selbst); that very question genau diese Frage; to worry about sich Sorgen machen um

APPENDIX

USEFUL CLASSROOM PHRASES

	Zur Begrüßung
Good morning/afternoon/evening.	Guten Morgen/Tag/Abend.
Hello. How are you (today)? – Fine, thanks. / Not so bad. What about you? / And you?	Hallo. Wie geht's (heute)? – Gut, danke. / Nicht schlecht. Und dir/Ihnen/euch?
	Zum Abschied
Goodbye./Bye.	(Auf) Wiedersehen.
Have a nice weekend. – Thank you. And the same to you.	Schönes Wochenende. – Danke, gleichfalls.
See you next week / on Thursday.	Bis nächste Woche / nächsten Donnerstag.
See you!	Tschüs!
	Um etwas bitten
(Sorry,) could I have a look at your Vocabulary Book?	Könnte ich mal bitte dein/Ihr Vokabelheft sehen?
(Excuse me,) could I borrow your Learner's Handbook for a moment?	Könnte ich mir mal kurz dein/Ihr Lernerhandbuch leihen?
Could I borrow a pen, please?	Könnte ich mir mal einen Stift ausleihen?
Could you give me a piece of paper, please?	Könntest du / Könnten Sie mir ein Blatt Papier geben?
	Für etwas danken
Thank you very much. – Not at all. / That's all right. / You're welcome.	Vielen Dank. – Nichts zu danken. / Keine Ursache.
	Sich entschuldigen
I'm sorry. – That's all right.	Entschuldigung. – Macht nichts.
I'm sorry I'm late.	Tut mir leid, daß ich zu spät komme.
I'm afraid I didn't have time to do my homework.	Ich hatte leider keine Zeit, meine Hausaufgaben zu machen.
I'm afraid I've forgotten my exercise book. – Don't worry about it. It doesn't matter.	Ich habe leider mein Heft zu Hause vergessen. – Macht nichts.
	Gute Wünsche
Bless you!	*(Jemand hat geniest.)* Gesundheit!
Good luck!	Viel Glück!
Have a good holiday/trip!	Schönen Urlaub / Gute Reise!
Have fun!	Viel Spaß!
Happy birthday!	Herzlichen Glückwunsch (zum Geburtstag)!
Merry Christmas!	Frohe Weihnachten!
Happy New Year / Easter!	Frohes Neues Jahr / Frohe Ostern!

Um Wiederholung bitten

Pardon?	Wie bitte?
Can you say that again?	Kannst du / Können Sie das nochmal sagen?
Can you explain that again?	Kannst du / Können Sie das nochmal erklären?
I'm sorry, what was that word again?	Wie war das Wort nochmal, bitte?
I'm sorry, what did you say?	Bitte, was hast du / haben Sie gesagt?
Could you please repeat what you said / the last word / the last sentence?	Könntest du / Könnten Sie bitte wiederholen, was Sie gesagt haben? / Könntest du / Könnten Sie das letzte Wort / den letzten Satz bitte wiederholen?
Could you say that again more slowly?	Könntest du / Könnten Sie das noch einmal langsamer sagen?

Bitten, daß jemand lauter/langsamer spricht

Could you speak louder, please? / Could you speak up, please?	Bitte, könntest du / könnten Sie lauter sprechen?
Please, could you speak more slowly?	Könntest du / Könnten Sie bitte langsamer sprechen?

Nachfragen, ob man richtig verstanden wurde

Do you see what I mean?	Verstehst du / Verstehen Sie, was ich meine?

Nachfragen, ob man richtig verstanden hat

Does that mean "speak" is an irregular verb?	Heißt das, „speak" ist ein unregelmäßiges Verb?

Zeit zum Nachdenken gewinnen

Well, let me see, what I like about Britain are the pubs.	Also, mal überlegen, was ich an England mag sind die Pubs.
I like folk music, you know, for example Joni Mitchell and James Taylor.	Ich mag Folkmusic, weißt du / wissen Sie, zum Beispiel Joni Mitchell und James Taylor.

Das Thema wechseln

Oh, by the way, …	Ach, übrigens, ...
Oh, before I forget, …	Ach, bevor ich's vergesse, ...

Nach der Aussprache eines Wortes fragen

How do you pronounce this word?	Wie spricht man dieses Wort aus?
Where is the stress in this word?	Wie ist bei diesem Wort die Betonung?
Do you say "…" or "…"?	Sagt man „..." oder „..."?

Nach der Schreibweise eines Wortes fragen

Can you spell that?	Kannst du / Können Sie das buchstabieren?
How do you spell "neighbour" in American English?	Wie schreibt man „neighbour" im amerikanischen Englisch?

Nachfragen, ob etwas korrekt ist

Is that right?	Ist das richtig?
Is it correct to say "…"	Ist es richtig, zu sagen „..."?

Sagen, daß etwas korrekt, bzw. nicht korrekt ist

Yes, that's correct/right.	Ja, das ist korrekt/richtig.
(Sorry,) that's not right.	Das ist (leider) nicht richtig.
(I'm afraid,) that's wrong.	Das ist (leider) falsch.
I don't think that's right.	Ich glaube nicht, daß das richtig ist.

	Nachfragen, wie ein bestimmtes Wort auf englisch oder auf deutsch heißt
What does "..." mean?	Was heißt „..."?
Does "..." mean "..." in German?	Heißt „..." auf deutsch „..."?
What's "..." in English?	Was heißt „..." auf englisch?
What's the English word/expression for "..."?	Was ist das englische Wort / der englische Ausdruck für „..."?
	Nachfragen, wie ein bestimmtes Wort verwendet wird
How do you use that word in a sentence?	Wie verwendet man das Wort in einem Satz?
Can you use that word in a sentence?	Können Sie / Kannst du das Wort in einem Satz verwenden?
	Sagen, daß man etwas nicht verstanden hat
(I'm sorry,) I don't understand.	(Tut mir leid,) ich verstehe das nicht.
I'm not sure I understood you (correctly).	Ich bin nicht sicher, ob ich Sie/dich (richtig) verstanden habe.
	Sagen, daß man etwas nicht weiß
I'm sorry. I don't know.	Tut mir leid, das weiß ich nicht.
	Sagen, daß man etwas vergessen hat
I'm afraid I can't remember the English word for "...".	Ich weiß leider das englische Wort für „..." nicht mehr.
I' ve forgotten what that word / "..." means in German.	Ich habe vergessen, was dieses Wort / „..." auf deutsch heißt.
	Sagen, daß jemand an der Reihe ist
It's your turn.	Sie sind / Du bist dran / an der Reihe.
It's Ingrid's turn.	Ingrid ist dran / an der Reihe.
	Fragen, wer an der Reihe ist
Whose turn is it?	Wer ist dran / an der Reihe?

TEST YOUR ENGLISH
ANSWER THE QUESTIONS
Here is my answer...
TASKS: 8,17,22,27,32,37,46
20
18
17
16
TELL THE TIME
TASKS: 11,16,26,48
14
13
12
11
SAY THE NUMBERS
SIXTY-EIGHT!
FIFTY-NINE!
TASKS: 4,9,23,35
9
8
ASK ANOTHER STUDENT
TASKS: 2,12,28,29,50

TASKS: 1, 10, 13, 33, 38, 49
VOCABULARY
Dictionary
21
22
24
FILL IN THE GAPS
This is an umbrella
I am from Dresden.
TASKS: 14, 15, 18, 25, 39, 40, 44
VERBS
BLA...BLA...BLA...
TASKS: 3, 19, 20, 31, 41, 45, 47
LONDON
27
28
29
SAY SOMETHING...
It's your turn!
TASKS: 5, 6, 7, 21, 24, 30, 34, 36, 42, 43
5
4
3
1
START
FINISH

Das alphabetische Wörterverzeichnis enthält den Wortschatz von Unit 1 bis Unit 12.

Wörter, die Sie nicht unbedingt zu lernen brauchen, sind ***kursiv*** gedruckt.

Die Zahlen geben an, wo die einzelnen Wörter und Wendungen zum ersten Mal vorkommen (z. B. **6/8.1** bedeutet Unit 6, Abschnitt 8.1)

Die neuen Wörter der *Options* finden Sie im *Vocabulary Book.*

Abkürzungen

AE American English
jd jemand
jdm jemandem
jdn jemanden
pl. plural
sb somebody *(jemand/-em/-en)*
sth something *(etwas)*

A

a ein/e **1/1; a, an** ein/e **2/1.1; 60 pence a pound** 60 Pence pro Pfund **5/1**
a lot of viele, viel **5/13.1**
about über, zu **3/5.2**; ungefähr **3/9; it's about** es geht um **10/6.1; what about ...?** was ist mit ...? **1/8.1**
activity Tätigkeit **6/8.1**
actually wirklich, tatsächlich **11/2.1**
address Adresse **4/3.2**
adult Erwachsene/r **8/2.1**
afraid: be afraid Angst haben, sich fürchten **12/1.1; I'm afraid** leider **11/3**
African afrikanisch **10/9.1**
after nach **4/5**
afternoon Nachmittag **1/4**
again wieder, noch einmal **4/1.2**
age Alter **6/11**
ago: a long time ago vor langer Zeit **12/1.2**
ahead (of) vor **6/10.4**
airline Fluggesellschaft **4/1.3**
ale Ale *(eine Art helles obergäriges Bier)* **10/9.1**
all alle **4/5**; alles **8/10.1; all day** den ganzen Tag **11/3; all over** überall (in) **10/9.1; all right** in Ordnung **5/7.2**
aloud laut **6/7.1**
also auch **9/1.2**
always immer **6/4.2**
am *von 0 bis 12 Uhr;* **10 am** 10 Uhr vormittags **6/10.3**
American Amerikaner/in, amerikanisch **1/8.3**
American Indian nordamerikanische/r Indianer/in **5/13.1**
anchovy Sardelle **9/1.2**
and und **1/1.2**
animal Tier **10/9.1**
another ein/e andere/r/s **7/4**
answer Antwort **2/8.2**; (be-)antworten **5/13.4**
answering machine Anrufbeantworter **10/6.1**
anything else? sonst noch etwas? **5/2.2**
apple Apfel **3/1.1**
apple pie *(englischer gedeckter)* Apfelkuchen **5/13.1**
approach sich nähern **12/8.1**
apricot Aprikose **5/1.1**
armchair Sessel **3/1.1**
arrange vereinbaren, ausmachen **11/2**
arrive ankommen **12/4.1**
artificial sweetener Süßstoff **8/4.4**
as wie **4/8.1**; als **8/10.1**
ashtray Aschenbecher **9/4**
ask fragen **3/5.2; ask sb (to do sth)** jdn bitten (etwas zu tun) **10/5.1**
assistant Verkäufer/in **5/10.1**
associate assoziieren **6/9.2**
at an, in **2/1.1**; bei **4/1.2**; um **5/13.1; at home** zu Hause **1/8.1; at school** in der Schule **2/1.1; at university** an der Universität **2/1.1; at the newsagent's** beim Zeitungshändler, im Zeitungsladen **5/6; at work** an der Arbeitsstelle; bei der Arbeit **8/3.1; at night** nachts **1/4; at nine o'clock** um neun Uhr **5/13.1; at the age of eleven** mit elf Jahren, im Alter von elf Jahren **6/11; at the weekend** am Wochenende **6/5.3**
at all: not ... at all überhaupt nicht, gar nicht **10/3.1**
at least mindestens **9/1.2**
at once gleichzeitig; sofort **8/10.1**
atmosphere Atmosphäre **10/9.1**
attend besuchen **6/11**
attractive attraktiv **3/10.1**
Austrian Österreicher/in, österreichisch **1/10.2**
automatic Maschinenpistole/-gewehr **12/8.1**
away weg **8/10.1**

B

back hinten **8/10.1**
bacon Schinkenspeck **8/1**
bad schlecht **5/11.1; that's too bad** das ist ja blöd/schlimm **11/3**
balcony Balkon **3/10.1**
banana Banane **5/1.1**
basket Korb **12/8.1**
bath-tub Badewanne **3/7.1**
bathroom Bad, Badezimmer **3/7.2**
be sein **1**
beach Strand **5/13.1**
beautiful schön **10/1**
bean Bohne **5/1.1**
because weil **5/13.1**
become werden **8/10.1**
bed Bett **3/7.1**
bedroom Schlafzimmer **3/7.2**
bedside table Nachttisch **3/7.1**
beep Piepton **10/6.1**
beer Bier **6/8.1**
before vorher, früher **12/3**; bevor **12/8.1**
behind hinter **3/5.1**
believe glauben **10/9.1**
best beste/r/s **3/10.2**; am besten, am liebsten **7/1.1**
between zwischen **3/5.1**
bicycle Fahrrad **6/8.1**
big groß **5/11.1**
birthday Geburtstag **9/1.2**
biscuit Keks **8/2.1**
black schwarz **6/9.2**
blackboard Tafel **11/5.1**
blue blau **5/4**; melancholisch **6/9.1**

blueberry Blaubeere **5/1.1**
board game Brettspiel **7/7**
book Buch **2/1.1**
bookcase Bücherregal **3/1.1**
boot Stiefel **6/1.1**
boring langweilig **5/11.1**
boss Chef/in **1/3**
both beide **8/10.1**
bottle Flasche **3/1.1;** ***bottled milk*** Milch in Flaschen **8/10.2**
bottle opener Flaschenöffner **9/4**
bowl Schüssel **8/3.1**
box Schachtel **5/6;** Kästchen **11/2.1**
boyfriend Freund **4/6.3**
bread Brot **8/1**
break (zer-)brechen **6/9.1**
breakfast Frühstück **6/1.1**
briefcase Aktentasche **7/7**
bring mitbringen **9/4.2;** bringen **12/4.1**
British britisch **3**
brother Bruder **4/1.2**
brown braun **5/4**
bun weiches Brötchen **9/4.2**
busy beschäftigt **1/1.2**
but aber **1/1.2;** sondern **12/8.1**
butter Butter **8/1**
buy kaufen **5/13.1**
by von **10/3.4**
bye tschüs, Wiedersehen **1/4**

C

cake Kuchen **8**
call Anruf, Gespräch,**10/5.3;** anrufen **10/6.1**
call back zurückrufen **10/5.1**
called: be called genannt werden, heißen **6/11**
can können **2/6.4**
canteen Kantine **6/11**
car Auto **6/5.2**
care: I don't care mir ist es egal **6/9.1**
Caribbean karibisch **10/9.1**
carrot Möhre, Karotte **5/1.1**
carry tragen, bringen **12/8.1**
carton Tüte **9/1.2**
castle Schloß **12/4.1**
cat Katze **1/13**
Central European Time mitteleuropäische Zeit **6/10.4**
centre Zentrum **5/13.1**
century Jahrhundert **5/13.1**
cereal Getreideflocken **8/1**
certainly sicherlich, natürlich **5/5.1**
chair Stuhl **2/5.2**
champagne Sekt **9/1.2**
change Abwechslung **5/13.1;** Veränderung **8/2.1**
character Person *(in einem Buch oder einer Geschichte)* **12/4.1**
chart Tabelle **8/3.1**
cheap billig **5/11.1**
check überprüfen, nachschlagen, kontrollieren **2/8.2**
cheerio tschüs **5/2.2**
cheese Käse **5/8.3**
cherry Kirsche **5/1.1**
chest of drawers Kommode **3/7.1**
chewing gum Kaugummi **5/6**
chicken Huhn, Hühnchen **5/8.3**
child *pl.* **children** Kind **1/8.1**
childhood Kindheit **12**
chocolate Schokolade, Praline **8/3.1**
choose (aus-)wählen **12/8.3**
cigarette Zigarette **5/6**
cinema Kino **5/13.1**
class Klasse **8.5**
classical music klassische Musik **10/3.1**
clean sauber **10/9.1;** saubermachen **12/4.1**
clock Uhr **6/10.2**
close schließen, zumachen **5/13.1**
clothes *pl.* Kleider, Kleidung **6/1.1**
clotted cream *(sehr dicker)* Rahm **8/7**
coast Küste **5/13.1**
coastline Küste **10/9.1**
coat Mantel **7/5.2**
coffee Kaffee **1/1.2**
coffee maker Kaffeemaschine **3/7.1**
coffee-table Couchtisch **3/1.1**
cold kalt **5/11.1**
collect sammeln **7/2.2**
colour Farbe **5/4**
combine kombinieren, verbinden **4/3.2**
come kommen **5/13.1**
come along vorbeikommen **12/8.1**
come in hereinkommen **1/1.2**
come out erscheinen, herauskommen **7/1.2**
comedy Komödie **10/2.1**
common gewöhnlich, normal **8/10.1**
company Firma, Unternehmen **7/1.2;** Gesellschaft **8/10.1**
compare vergleichen
comparison Vergleich **12/8.2**
complete vervollständigen, ausfüllen **3/5.1**
comprehensive school Gesamtschule **6/11**
computer programmer EDV-Programmierer/in **4/1.2**
container Behälter, Gefäß **9**
continental breakfast kleines Frühstück **8/1**
continental-type breakfast eine Art kleines Frühstück **8/2.1**
conversation Gespräch **4/1.2**
cook kochen **6/1.1;** Koch/Köchin **12/7**
cooker Herd **3/7.1**
corkscrew Korkenzieher **9/4**
correct korrekt, richtig **2/8.2;** korrigieren **5/13.2**
cosmetics Kosmetikartikel, Schönheitspflegemittel **5/13.1**
cosmopolitan kosmopolitisch, international **10/9.1**
could könnte/n **8/10.1;** konnte/n **12/4.1**
council house Sozialwohnung **3/9**
country Land **2/1.1**
country home Landhaus **10/9.1**
countryside Landschaft, Land **10/9.1**
cousin Cousin/e **4/7**
cream Rahm **9/1.2**
crisp (Kartoffel-)Chip **2/8.2**
cross out ausstreichen **11/7.1**
crossword puzzle Kreuzworträtsel **2/7**
crustless ohne Kruste **8/7**
cucumber (Salat-)Gurke **5/1.1**
culture Kultur **10/9.3**
cup Tasse **1/1.2**
cupboard (Küchen-)Schrank **3/7.1**
customer Kunde/Kundin **5/3**

D

dad Vati, Papa **6/5.3**
daily täglich **3/7.2**
dance tanzen **10/3.4**

dancer Tänzer/in **1/11**
dark dunkel **8/10.1**
daughter Tochter **4/1.2**
dawn Dämmerung, Morgengrauen **8/10.1**
day Tag **4/7**
dead tot **12/4.1**
dear ... liebe/r... *(Anredeform im Brief)* **4/7**; mein/e Liebe/r *(informelle Anrede)* **5/3**
deliver liefern **8/10.2**
department store Kaufhaus **5/13.1**
depend abhängen; **it depends** es hängt davon ab, es kommt darauf an **8/3.1**
describe beschreiben **3/3**
description Beschreibung **3/8**
desk Schreibtisch **3/1.1**
detached house *(freistehendes)* Einfamilienhaus **3/9**
detective film Krimi, Kriminalfilm **10/2.1**
dialogue Dialog **5/5.1**
dictionary Wörterbuch **3/1.1**
different verschieden, unterschiedlich **5/11.2**; anders **12/1.1**
difficult schwierig **5/12**
dining room Eßzimmer **3/10.1**
dinner *(Hauptmahlzeit)* Mittag- *oder* Abendessen **8/7**
disappear verschwinden **12/8.1**
disciplined diszipliniert **10/9.1**
disgusting ekelhaft, widerlich **6/5.2**
dish Schüssel, Schale **12/4.1**; **dishes** *pl.* Geschirr **12/7**; **do the dishes** das Geschirr spülen **12/7**
dishwasher Geschirrspülmaschine **3/7.1**
dislike nicht mögen **10/3.1**
dislikes *pl.* Abneigungen **10**
district Bezirk **6/10.4**
divorced geschieden **4/1.2**
do tun, machen **1/7**
doctor Arzt/Ärztin **1/8.1**
documentary Dokumentarfilm **10/2.1**
dog Hund **1/13**
door Tür **1/13**
double doppelt, Doppel- **2/5.3**
dozen Dutzend **5/8.3**
dream Traum **7/1.1**
dress Kleid **12/4.1**
drink Getränk **5/11.2**; trinken **6/1.1**; **go for a drink** etwas trinken gehen **11/3**
drive fahren **7/2.1**
driving (das) Autofahren **10/9.1**
drop fallen lassen **12/4.1**
drugstore AE Drogeriemarkt, Drugstore **5/13.1**
duck/ducky Ente; junger Mann, junge Frau *(informelle Anrede)* **5/3**
during während **7/5.2**
dwarf Zwerg **12/4.1**

E

each jede/r/s (einzelne); **25 pence each** 25 Pence das Stück **5/1.1**
ear Ohr **12/4.1**
early früh **8/10.2**
east Osten **5/13.3**
easy leicht **12/8.1**
eat essen **6/8.1**
eating habits *pl.* Eßgewohnheiten **8/2**
egg Ei **5/8.3**
either: either ... or entweder ... oder **8/3.1**; **not ... either** auch nicht **10**
empty leer **2/5.2**
end Ende **8/10.1**; schließen, enden **8/7**
ending Endung **3/2.1**
English Engländer/in, englisch **1/10.2**; ***English-speaking*** englischsprachig **2/1.1**; **Englishman** Engländer, **Englishwoman** Engländerin **10/9.3**
enough genug **7/5.2**
entertaining unterhaltsam **10/1**
equivalent Entsprechung **8/9**
ethnic ethnisch **10/9.1**
even sogar **10/9.1**; selbst **12/8.1**
evening Abend **1/4**
every jede/r/s **4/1.2**
everything alles **9/1.2**
example Beispiel **10/9.1**
exercise Übung **5/12**
exercise book Heft **3/1.1**
expensive teuer **5/11.1**
explain erklären **7/5.1**
expression Ausdruck, Wendung **5/13.3**
eye Auge **12/1.1**

F

fable Fabel **12/8**
fact Tatsache **8/2.1**
fairy Fee **12/4.1**; ***fairy tale*** Märchen **12/4**
fall fallen **12/5.2**; **fall apart** auseinanderfallen **6/9.1**; **fall asleep** einschlafen **12/7**; **fall in love with** sich verlieben in **12/4.1**
false falsch **5/13.2**
family Familie **1/10.4**
famous berühmt **5/13.1**
farmer Bauer **12/1.1**
fast schnell **5/13.1**
fast food Fast Food, Schnellimbiß-Kost **5/13.1**
father Vater **1/8.1**
favourite Lieblings- **5/13.1**; Favorit **7/1.1**
feel fühlen **8/10.1**; sich fühlen **11/3**
fetch abholen **7/2.1**
fill in ausfüllen, eintragen **3/1.1**
finally endlich, schließlich **12/8.1**
find finden **4/8.1**
fine gut **1/1.2**; in Ordnung **5/10.1**
finish zu Ende sein, enden **6/1.1**
fireplace (offener) Kamin **3/1.1**
firm Firma, Unternehmen **4/1.2**
first erste/r/s **1/3**; zuerst **6/5.1**
first name Vorname **1/3**
fitted eingebaut **3/10.1**
flash card Karteikarte **1/9**
flat Wohnung **3/9**
florist Blumenhändler/in **5/7.2**
fog Nebel **10/9.1**
follow folgen **8/7**
following folgend **5/5.1**
food Essen **5/13.1**
fool zum Narren halten, hereinlegen **12/8.1**
foot *pl.* **feet** Fuß *(Maß): 1 foot = 30,48 cm* **12/8.1**
football Fußball **6/5.3**
for für, zu **2/1.1**; für, bei **4/1.2**; denn **12/8.1**; **for a week** eine Woche lang **5/13.1**; **for example** zum Beispiel **10/9.1**
foreigner Ausländer/in **10/9.1**
forest Wald **12/4.1**
fork Gabel **9/4**
forlorn verlassen, verloren **8/10.1**
form bilden **7/2.2**

free frei, kostenlos **10/5.1**; ***free-range egg*** Freilandei **5/8.3**
freezer Gefrierschrank, Kühltruhe **3/7.1**
French französisch **2/7**
French champagne Champagner **9/1.2**
Friday Freitag **6**
fried egg Spiegelei **8/1**
friend Freund/in **2/1.1**
friendly freundlich **10/9.1**
from aus **1/7.1**; von **7/2.1**; **from ... to ...** von ... bis ... **6/10.3**
front: in front of vor **3/5.1**
frozen gefroren, tiefgekühlt **5/8.3**
fruit Obst, Frucht **5/1.1**
full voll **5/11.1**; komplett **8/1**
full-cream milk Vollmilch **8/2.1**
fully-fitted kitchen (komplette) Einbauküche **3/10.1**
fun Spaß **5/13.1**; **it's fun** es macht Spaß **5/13.1**
funny komisch, lustig **10/1**; seltsam **12/7**
furnished möbliert **3/10.1**
furniture Möbel **3/7.2**

G

game Spiel **6/7**
gap Lücke **10/7.2**
garbage can AE Mülleimer **1/13**
garden Garten **4/1.2**
gay *hier:* fröhlich **8/10.1**
genie Geist **12/4.1**
German Deutsche/r, deutsch **1/10.2**
get bekommen **5/13.1**; werden **6/4.2**; holen, besorgen, kaufen **9/1.2**; **get married** heiraten **12/4.1**
get together sich treffen, zusammenkommen **11/5.2**
get up aufstehen **6/5.2**
girl Mädchen **12**
girlfriend Freundin **4/1.2**
give geben **6/8.3**
glass Glas **3/1.1**; **glasses** *pl.* Brille **6/8.1**
go gehen, fahren **2/1.1**; **go on holiday** Ferien/Urlaub machen **2/1.1**; **go to university** zur Universität gehen, studieren **4/1.2**
go away weggehen/-fahren **8/10.1**

good gut **1/4**; **good morning** guten Morgen **1/4**
goodbye auf Wiedersehen **1/4**
grammar school Gymnasium **6/11**
granddad Großpapa, Opa **4/7**
grandmother Großmutter **6/8.4**
grandparents Großeltern **4/7**
granny Großmama, Oma **4/7**
great großartig, toll **4/1.2**
green grün **5/4**
Greenwich Mean Time (GMT) westeuropäische Zeit **6/10.4**
grey grau **6/9.1**
groove sich mitreißen lassen, es sich gut gehen lassen **9/1.1**
group Gruppe **7/1.1**
guess raten, erraten **2/3**
guitar Gitarre **7/1.1**

H

habit Gewohnheit **6**
half Hälfte, halb; **half past seven** halb acht **6/5.2**; **half a litre** ein halber Liter **8/2.1**
ham Schinken **8/7**
handbag Handtasche **7/5.2**
handkerchief Taschentuch **7/5.2**
handsome gutaussehend **10/1**
happy glücklich **12/1.1**
hard-boiled hartgekocht **8/4.4**
hate hassen **6/5.2**
have haben **1/8.1**; essen **8/2.1**; trinken **8/2.1**; **have a drink** etwas trinken (gehen) **11/1.1**; **have a party** eine Party geben/feiern; **have breakfast** frühstücken **6/5.2**; **have lunch** zu Mittag essen **6/10.5**; **have supper** zu Abend essen **7/2.1**
have sth on etwas anhaben, tragen **12/8.1**
hear hören **10/3.3**
heart Herz **6/9.1**
hello hallo, (guten) Tag **1/1.2**; ***hello there*** na, hallo **11/1.1**
help helfen **6/5.3**
hesitate zögern **6/9.1**
here hier **1/1.2**; **here you are** bitte sehr **5/2.2**
hi hallo, grüß dich / grüßt euch **1/4**
high tea *Kombination aus Nachmittagstee und Abendessen* **8/7**
historical historisch **10/9.1**
history Geschichte **10/9.1**

holiday(s) Urlaub, Ferien **2/1.1**
homework Hausaufgaben **6/5.3**
home Zuhause, Heim **1/7.1**; nach Hause, heim **6/1.1**
honey Honig **8/1**
hope Hoffnung **8/10.1**; hoffen **5/13.1**;
horrible schrecklich, fürchterlich **10/1**
hot heiß **5/11.1**
hour Stunde **5/13.1**
house Haus **1/13**; ***house-husband*** Hausmann; **1/8.1**; ***housewife*** *pl.* ***housewives*** Hausfrau **1/8.3**
how? wie? **1**; **how many?** wie viele? **9**; **how much?** wieviel? **5/2.2**; **how are you?** wie geht es dir/Ihnen? **1**; **how do you do?** guten Tag/Abend; angenehm **1/4**
hungry hungrig **12/4.1**
husband (Ehe-)Mann **1/8.1**

I

I'd like = I would like ich würde gern **11/1.1**
I'd love = I would love ich würde sehr gern **11/1.1**
idea Idee **11/1.1**
idiom idiomatische Wendung, Redewendung **8/9**
if ob **6/9.1**; wenn, falls **7/5**
imagine (sth) sich (etwas) vorstellen **11/5.2**
important wichtig **10/9.1**
in in **1/7.1**; **in here** hier drinnen **1/1.2**; **in the photo** auf dem Foto **4/1.2**; **she's not in** sie ist nicht zu Hause **10/5.1**; **in the afternoon** nachmittags **1/4**; **in the evening** abends **1/4**; **in the morning** morgens **1/4**; **in one day** innerhalb von einem Tag **10/9.1**; **in German** auf deutsch **1/10.2**; **in love** verliebt **6**; **in the end** schließlich, am Schluß **12/4.1**
independent unabhängig **6/11**
interesting interessant **5/11.1**
interior decoration Innenausstattung, Einrichtung **10/9.1**
interview interviewen, befragen **7/4**
introduce vorstellen **1/2**

invite einladen **10/9.1**
Irish Ire/Irin, irisch **1/10.2**
Italian italienisch **10/9.1**

J

jam Marmelade, Konfitüre **8/1**
jar Glas **9/1.2**
job Beruf **1/8.1**
juice Saft **8/1**
jumbled durcheinander(-geworfen) **8**
June Juni **10/9.1**
just nur, bloß **8/10.1**; einfach **9/1.2**; ***just fine*** ganz gut **1/1.2**; **just a moment** Moment mal, einen Moment **10/5.1**

K

key Schlüssel **3/1.1**
kill töten **12/4.1**
kind Art, Sorte **10/2**
king König **12/4.1**
kitchen Küche **3/7.2**
knife *pl.* **knives** Messer **7/5.1**
know wissen **6/5.4**; kennen **9/3.2**

L

lamp Lampe **3/1.1**
language Sprache **2/1.1**
large groß **3/10.1**
last letzte/r/s **9/1.2**; dauern **6/11**
late spät **6/9.1**
Latin music lateinamerikanische Musik **10/3.1**
lawn Rasen **10/9.1**
lawyer Rechtsanwalt/Rechtsanwältin **7/2.1**
lb *Abkürzung für* **pound** Pfund *(Gewichtseinheit)* **5/1**
learn lernen **1/9**
leave weggehen **12/4.1**; hinterlassen **10/6.1**
left übrig **8/10.1**; **left-over** übrig geblieben **9/1.2**
lemon Zitrone **5/1.1**
let lassen **9**; **let's = let us** laß uns / lassen Sie uns / laßt uns **9**; **let's see** warte mal, laß mich mal überlegen **9/1.2**
letter Brief **2/1.1**
lettuce Kopfsalat **8/7**
lie liegen **5/13.1**
life *pl.* **lives** Leben **5/13.1**
like wie **10/9.1**; **like this** genauso wie hier **7/2.2**
like mögen **2/1.1**
likes *pl.* Vorlieben **10**
lion Löwe **12/8.1**
lipstick Lippenstift **7/5.2**
list Liste **4/3.2**
listen (zu-)hören; **listen to the radio** Radio hören **2/1.1**
litre Liter **8/2.1**
little klein **10/9.1**; wenig **4/7**
live wohnen, leben **3/9**
living room Wohnzimmer **3/1**
loaf *pl.* **loaves** Laib **9/1.12**
lobster Hummer **5/13.1**
local authorities Gemeindeverwaltung **3/9**
lonely einsam **8/10.1**
long lang **1/10.1**
longitude Länge **6/10.4**
look aussehen **4/1.2**; **look at** anschauen, ansehen **3/8**
lots of viele, viel **4/7**
love lieben, sehr mögen **4/8.1**; Liebe **4/8.1**; Geliebte/r **8/10.1**; meine Liebe, mein Lieber *(informelle Anrede)* **5/2.2**; **love, ...** dein/e ... *(Schlußformel beim Brief)* **4/7**
lunch Mittagessen **6/10.5**
luxury Luxus-, luxuriös **3/10.1**
lyrics *pl.* Text

M

madam meine Dame *(formelle Anrede)* **5/3**
main Haupt- **3/9**; **main meal** Hauptmahlzeit **8/2.1**
make machen, bilden **4/3.2**; **make friends** Freundschaften schließen **10/9.1**
make up bilden **7/1.2**
man Mann **4/6.3**
many viele **5/13.1**
March März **6/10.4**
mark markieren, ankreuzen **3/2.1**
market Markt **5**
marmalade *Marmelade aus Zitrusfrüchten* **8/1**
marry heiraten **12/4.1**
match Streichholz **3/1.1**
match with zuordnen, das Passende (zu etwas) finden **3/1.1**
matter: what's the matter? was ist los? **11/3**
meal Mahlzeit, Essen **6/5.2**
mean armselig **8/10.1**
mean bedeuten **7/5.1**; meinen **7/5.1**
meaning Bedeutung **2/3**
meat Fleisch **6/8.1**
medicine Medizin, Arznei **5/13.1**
meet treffen **10/6.1**; sich treffen **11/1.1**; kennenlernen **1/1.2**
meeting Treffen **1/6**
melon Melone **5/1.1**
member Mitglied **7/1.1**
memory Erinnerung **12**
message Nachricht, Mitteilung **8/10.1**
microwave Mikrowelle **3/7.1**
midday Mittag **8/7**
midnight Mitternacht **12/4.1**
mile Meile *(= 1,6 km)* **5/13.1**
milk Milch **8**
mind: I don't mind ... ich habe nichts gegen ... **10/1**
mineral water Mineralwasser **9/1.2**
mirror Spiegel **3/7.1**
miss verpassen, versäumen **5/8.3**
missing fehlend **3/2.2**
mix Mischung **10/9.1**
Monday Montag **6/9.1**
money Geld **7/5.2**
month Monat **7/1.2**
more mehr; **two more ...** noch zwei ... **6/8.1**
morning Morgen **1/4**
most die meisten **3/9**
mother Mutter **1/8.1**
move umziehen **7/1.2**; sich bewegen **9/1.1**
movie AE Film **5/13.1**
movie theater AE Kino **5/13.1**
much viel **9/1.2**
mushroom Pilz, Champignon **5/1.1**
music Musik **7/1.1**
musician Musiker/in **7/1.1**
must müssen **6/11**
mustard Senf **9/4.2**

N

napkin Serviette **9/4**
near nahe (bei), in der Nähe von **3/10.1**
necessary nötig, notwendig **8/1**
need brauchen **2/1.1**
neighbour Nachbar/in **4/1.2**
never nie **6/9.1**
new neu **2/3**
news *pl.* Nachrichten **7/2.1**
newsagent Zeitungshändler/in **5/6**
newspaper Zeitung **2/7**
next nächste/r/s **4/7; next to** neben **3/5.1; next, please** der/die Nächste bitte **5/2.2**
nice nett, schön **1/4**
night Nacht **1/4**
nightcap Nachthaube, Schlafmütze **12/8.1**
nightgown Nachthemd **12/8.1**
no nein **1/8.3**; kein/e **8/10.1**; nicht **12/8.1; no one** niemand, keiner **9/4.2**
nobody niemand, keiner **2/5.2**
nonsense Unsinn **12.7**
nor auch nicht **10**
normally normalerweise **8/2.1**
north Norden **5/13.3**
nose Nase **12/4.1**
not nicht **1/8.3; not at all** bitte sehr **5/7.2; *not even*** (noch) nicht einmal **6/9.1; *not ... any more*** nicht mehr **12/8.1**
note Notiz **10/2.1; take notes** Notizen machen **10/2.1**
notepad Notizblock **7/5.2**
nothing nichts **12/7**
now jetzt, nun **1/1.2; *now then*** na **1/1.2**
nowadays heutzutage **12/8.1**
number Zahl, Nummer **2/5**

O

0 [əʊ] Null **2/5.3**
occasionally gelegentlich, manchmal **8/3.1**
o'clock: at 9 o'clock um 9 Uhr **5/13.1**
October Oktober **6/10.4**
of von **2/3**
of course selbstverständlich, natürlich **7/1.1**
offer Angebot **5/8.3**; anbieten **10/9.1**
office Büro **7/2.1**
often oft **8/3.1**
OK okay, in Ordnung **5/7.2**
old alt **4/1.2**
on auf **3/1.1**; an **5/13.1; on holiday** im Urlaub, in den Ferien **2/1.1; on television** im Fernsehen **7/2.1; a new film is on at the cinema** ein neuer Film läuft im Kino **11/1.1; on Saturdays** samstags **6/5.3; on Monday** (am) Montag **6/10.5**
one: the ones die(jenigen) **10/2.1**
onion Zwiebel **5/1.1**
only nur **3/9**
open öffnen, aufmachen **5/13.1**; offen, geöffnet **5/13.1**; offen, aufrichtig **10/9.1**
open up aufmachen **12/4.1**
opera Oper **10/3.1**
opposite Gegenteil **7/7**
or oder **1/12**
other andere/r/s **2/1.1**
outside außerhalb **6/11**
over there dort drüben/hinten **5/10.1**
own besitzen **3/9**
owner Besitzer/in **12/4.1**

P

packet Packung, Päckchen **5/6**
page Seite **3/1.1**
painter Maler/in **1/8.1**
Pakistani pakistanisch **10/9.1**
palace Palast **8/10.1**
pants *pl.* AE Hosen **1/13**
paper Papier **7/2.2**
parents Eltern **1/8.1**
part Teil **4/1.3**
part-time Teilzeit **7/2.1**
pass by vorbeigehen **8/10.1**
pass through verlaufen durch **6/10.4**
past nach; **half past eight** halb neun **6/5.2**
pastry Gebäck(-teilchen) **8/7**
pay (be-)zahlen **3/10.1**
pea Erbse **5/1.1**
peach Pfirsich **5/1.1**
pear Birne **5/1.1**
pen Füllfederhalter **3/1.1**
pence (p) Pence *(brit. Währung: 100 p = £1)* **5/1**
people Leute **2/1.1**
pepper Pfeffer **8/1**
per pro **3/10.1**
per cent Prozent **3/9**
personal persönlich **1/8**
pet Haustier, Haus- **6/1.1**
phone = telephone Telefon **2/5**
phonecard Telefonkarte **5/6**
photograph Foto **3/1.1**
phrase Redewendung **5/5**
pick up (ab-)holen **10/6.1**
picture Bild **3/1.1**
piece Stück **7/2.2**
pineapple Ananas **5/1.1**
pink rosa **6/9.2**
pipe Pfeife **6/8.1**
place Ort **8/10.1**
plan planen **9/4.1**
plant Pflanze **3/1.1**; pflanzen **5/13.1**
plate Teller **9/4**
play spielen **6/5.3**
please bitte **1/1.2**
pleased erfreut **1/1.2**
pleasure Spaß, Vergnügen **2/1.1**
plum Pflaume **5/1.1**
pm *von 12 bis 24 Uhr;* **3 pm** 3 Uhr nachmittags **6/10.3**
pocket calculator Taschenrechner **7/5.2**
poisoned vergiftet **12/4.1**
poor arm **12/4.1**
popular beliebt **8/2.2**
porridge Porridge, Haferbrei **8/1**
possible möglich **12/1.3**
potato Kartoffel **5/1.1**
pound (£) Pfund *(brit. Währung)* **3/10.2**; Pfund *(Gewichtseinheit)* **5/1**
practice Übung, Training **4/3**
practise üben **6/10.2**
prefer bevorzugen, lieber mögen, **7/1.1**
prepare vorbereiten, zubereiten **7/2.1**
president Präsident **4/3.2**
price Preis **5/1.1**
primary school Grundschule **6/11**
prime minister Premierminister/in **10/5.3**
prince Prinz **12/4.1**
pronounce aussprechen **7/5.1**
pronunciation Aussprache **1/5**
pub Kneipe **6/8.3**

public öffentlich **6/11**
public school Privatschule **6/11**
pupil Schüler/in **12/1.2**
purple violett **6/9.2**
purse Portemonnaie **7/5.2**
put on anziehen **12/4.1**

Q

quarter Viertel (Pfund) **5/10.1; a quarter to four** Viertel vor vier **6/5.2**
queen Königin **6/8.3**
question Frage **3/5.2**

R

rarely selten **8/3.1**
raspberry Himbeere **5/1.1**
read lesen **2/1.1**
reader Leser/in **12/8.2**
ready, steady, go! auf die Plätze, fertig, los! **2/8**
real echt, wirklich, richtig **10/9.1**
realistic realistisch **10/2.2**
really wirklich **1/8.1;** tatsächlich **6/11**
reason Grund, Ursache **8/10.1**
reception room *förmlich:* Wohnzimmer **3/10.1**
record Schallplatte **7/1.2**
red rot **5/4**
refrigerator Kühlschrank **3/7.1**
regards to ... Grüße an ... **5/13.1**
reign herrschen **8/10.1**
relative Verwandte/r **2/1.1**
relaxed entspannt, ruhig **10/9.1**
remember sich erinnern an **12/1.1**
rent Miete **3/10.1**
repeat wiederholen **4/8.1**
report to sb jdm berichten **10/2.1**
respond reagieren, antworten **11/4.1**
reverse roles die Rollen tauschen **5/6**
revision Wiederholung **10/4**
rewrite neu schreiben **12/8.3**
rhyme Reim **12/7**
rich reich **12/4.1**
ride fahren **6/8.1**
right richtig, korrekt **1/8.1;** gut, okay **11/2.1; *right now*** in diesem Augenblick, zur Zeit **10/3.4**
roll Brötchen **8/1**
romance Liebesgeschichte **8/10.1; *romance film*** Liebesfilm **10/2.1**
romantic romantisch **8/4.2**
room Raum, Zimmer **3/1**
rose Rose **10/9.1**
rug Teppich **3/7.1**
run rennen, laufen **12/5.2**
run away wegrennen/-laufen **12/4.1**

S

sad traurig **6/4.2**
safe sicher **10/9.1**
salad Salat **8/7**
salt Salz **8/1**
same: the same der/die/das gleiche(n) **10/3.1; *same to you*** gleichfalls **11/3**
satisfy befriedigen, zufriedenstellen **9/1.1**
Saturday Samstag **6/5.3**
saucer Untertasse **3/1.1**
sausage Wurst **8/1**
say sagen **6/2**
scarf *pl.* **scarves** Schal
school Schule **2/1.1**
scone *brötchenartiges Buttergebäck* **8/7**
Scottish Schotte/Schottin, schottisch **1/10.2**
scrambled egg Rührei **8/4.4**
sea Meer, (die) See **5/13.1**
seafood Meeresfrüchte **5/13.1**
second zweite/r/s **7/1.2**
secondary school Höhere Schule **6/11**
secret Geheimnis **6/7.1**
secretary Sekretär/in **1/7.1**
section Abschnitt **4/5**
seem scheinen **8/10.1**
see sehen **5/13.1;** verstehen **7/5.1**
sell sich verkaufen **8/9**
semi-detached house halbes Doppelhaus **3/9**
send schicken **9/1.1**
send out hinausschicken, losschicken **12/4.1**
sentence Satz **4/1.3**
separate getrennt **3/10.1**
serve servieren **9/1.2**
shelf *pl.* **shelves** Regal **3/1.1**
shirt Hemd **1/13**
shoot schießen**12/8.1**
shop Geschäft, Laden **5/3**
shopper Käufer/in **5/8.3**
shopping (das) Einkaufen **5/4; do one's shopping** seine Einkäufe erledigen/machen **5/13.2**
short kurz **1/10.1**
should sollte/n **9/1.2**
show zeigen **8/2.1**
shower Dusche **3/7.1**
sight Anblick **8/10.1**
silver silbern **12/4.1**
sing singen **6/8.1**
singer Sänger/in **6/9.2**
singing singend **7/1.2**
sink Spülbecken, Waschbecken **3/7.1**
sir mein Herr *(formelle Anrede)* **5/3**
sister Schwester **4/1.3**
slave Sklave **12/4.1**
sleep Schlaf **6/8.1;** schlafen **5/13.1**
slice Scheibe, Schnitte, Stück **9/1.2**
small klein **4/8.1**
smoke rauchen **6/8.1**
snow Schnee **10/9.1**
so also **1/10.2;** auch **10; so that** so daß, damit **8/10.2**
soft-boiled weichgekocht **8/4.4**
some einige **5/13.1;** etwas, ein bißchen **8/3.1; some more** noch einige **6/9.2**
somebody jemand **1/2; somebody else** jemand anders **12/4.1**
something etwas **10/2.1**
sometimes manchmal **4/1.2**
son Sohn **4/1.2**
song Lied **2/1.1**
soon bald **5/13.1**
sorry: I'm sorry es tut mir leid **7/5.1**
soul Seele **9/1.1**
sound Laut **8/8.2;** klingen **11/1.1**
south Süden **5/13.3; south-east** Südost(-) **6/10.4**
Spanish spanisch **10/7.3**
speak sprechen **2/1.1**
special offer Sonderangebot **5/8.3**
spell buchstabieren **2/6.4**
spend verbringen **10/9.1**
spoon Löffel **7/5.1**
stand stehen **8/10.1**

start Anfang, Beginn 8/10.1; anfangen, beginnen 4/1.2
start off anfangen 6/4.2
state school system staatliches Schulsystem 6/11
statement Behauptung, Aussage 8/2.2
stay bleiben 1/8.1; **stay with** wohnen bei 12/4.1
stepmother Stiefmutter 12/4.1
stepsister Stiefschwester 12/4.1
stereo Stereoanlage 3/1.1
still noch 6/11
stop anhalten 7/2.1
store AE Geschäft, Laden 5/13.1
storm Gewitter, Sturm 8/9
story 6/4.2
strawberry Erdbeere 5/1.1
street Straße 2/6.4
stress Betonung 2/4
student Student/in 1/11; Studierende/r, Lernende/r 7/4
studio Atelier 1/8.1
studio apartment Einzimmerwohnung 3/10.1
study Arbeitszimmer 3/8; lernen 11/5.2; **studies** *pl.* Studium 2/1.1
suddenly plötzlich 12/1.1
sugar Zucker 8/1
suggestion Vorschlag 11
summary Zusammenfassung 12/1.3
summer Sommer 4/1.2
sun Sonne 5/13.1
Sunday Sonntag 6/5.3
supermarket Supermarkt 5/13.1
supper Abendessen 7/2.1
surprise Überraschung(s-) 12/8.3
survey Untersuchung, Umfrage 8/2.1
swim schwimmen 5/13.1
swimming-pool Schwimmbad 4/7
Swiss Schweizer/in, schweizerisch 1/10.2
switchboard operator Telefonist/in 11/1.1

T

table Tisch 3/7.1; Tabelle 4/5
take nehmen, wegnehmen 8/9; **take a long time** lange dauern 10/9.1
take out herausnehmen/-holen 12/4.1
talk Gespräch 10/5; **talk about** reden, sprechen über 4/6; **talk to** sprechen, reden mit 6/5.1
tall story Übertreibung, Lügengeschichte 6/1.1; = ***tall tale*** AE 12/7
tape (Kassetten-)Band 6/3.2
taxi driver Taxifahrer/in 7/4.2
tea Tee 6/7.1
teacher Lehrer/in 1/8.1
team Mannschaft, Team 2/8
teapot Teekanne 3/1.1
teacup Teetasse 8/9
teaspoon Teelöffel 9/4
telephone Telefon 4/3.2
television Fernsehapparat 3/1.1; Fernsehen 6/4.1
tell (about) erzählen (von) 5/13.1; **tell sb to do sth** jdm sagen, daß er/sie etwas tun soll 12/4.1
terraced house Reihenhaus 3/9
test testen 7/7
than als 12/8.1
thank you danke 1/4; **thank you very much** vielen Dank 5/7.2; **thanks** danke 1/1.2; **thanks a lot** vielen Dank 5/7.2
that das 1/10.2; das (da/dort), jene/r/s 4/1.2; *(Relativpronomen:)* der/die/das, welche/r/s 10/3.4; daß 8/2.1; **that (one)** der/die/das (da), jene/r/s (dort) 5
the der/die/das 1/4
theatre Theater 5/13.1
then dann 1/1.2; damals 12/1.1; also 6/5.2
there dort, da 1/6; dahin, dorthin 4/1.2; **there is/are** dort ist/sind, es gibt 3; **there's** = **there is** dort/da ist 1/6
these diese, die (hier) 5
thin dünn 8/7
thing Ding, Sache 3/7.2
think denken, glauben 4/1.2; **think of** halten von, denken über 10/1
this dies, das 1/1.2; dies/das (hier) 4/1.2; **this (one)** der/die/das (hier), diese/r/s (hier) 5; **this afternoon** heute Nachmittag 10/5.1
those jene, die (dort) 5
through durch 6/10.4
Thursday Donnerstag 6/9.1
tick abhaken 11/2.1
time Zeit 4/7; **what time is it?** wieviel Uhr ist es? 6/8.1; ***time of day*** Tageszeit 12/1.1
tin (Konserven-)Dose 5/8.3
to zu 6/1.1; nach 2/1.1; bis 6/10.3; vor 6/5.2; **five to nine** fünf vor neun 6/5.2
today heute 5/8.3; ***today's*** der/die/das heutige 12/8.2
together zusammen 7/1.1
toilet Toilette 3/7.1
tomato Tomate 5/1.1
tomorrow morgen 7/5.2; **tomorrow morning** morgen früh 9/1.2
tonight heute abend 7/1.2
too auch 1/4; zu 6/9.1
tooth *pl.* **teeth** Zahn 12/4.1
touch berühren 5/1.1
tower Turm 4/7
town Stadt 8/10.1
traditional traditionell 8/2.1
traffic Verkehr 10/9.3
translate übersetzen 10/6.2
travel documents Reiseunterlagen 10/6.1
tree Baum 1/13
true richtig, wahr 5/13.2
try versuchen, probieren 5/5.1
try on anprobieren 12/4.1
Tuesday Dienstag 6/9.1
turn into verwandeln in 8/10.1
TV = **television** Fernsehen 6/5.3
two-up two-down kleines Reihenhäuschen 8/10.1
type Typ, Art 3/9
typical typisch 7/2.1

U

Ugh! igitt 6/1.1
ugly häßlich 10/1
umbrella Schirm 3/1.1
under unter 3/5.1
underline unterstreichen 3/4.1
understand verstehen 2/1.1
unfurnished unmöbiliert 3/10.1
unhappy unglücklich 12/1.1
unit Einheit, Lektion 1
university Universität 2/1.1
until bis 6/11
up here hier hoch, hier rauf 5/13.1

up-to-date aktuell 12/8.1
use Gebrauch, Verwendung 3/7.2; benutzen, verwenden, gebrauchen 1/9
used: as it used to be wie es früher war 12/8.1
useful nützlich
usually normalerweise 7/5.2

V

vacation AE Urlaub, Ferien 5/13.1; **on vacation** AE im Urlaub 5/13.1
various verschieden 8/7
vegetable Gemüse 5/1.1
very sehr 4/1.2; **very much** sehr 4/1.2
video Videogerät 3/1.1
village Dorf 10/9.1
violent gewalttätig 10/2.2
visit Besuch 1/1; besuchen 10/7.3
vocabulary Vokabular 7/6

W

wait (ab-)warten 5/13.1; **wait for** warten auf 12/8.1
wake (auf-)wecken 7/2.1
wake up aufwachen 7/2.1
walk Spaziergang 5/13.1; **take a walk** einen Spaziergang machen 5/13.1
want wollen 2/1.1
war Krieg 12/1.1
wardrobe Kleiderschrank 3/7.1
washing-machine Waschmaschine 3/7.1
watch Armbanduhr 7/5.2
watch (an-)sehen, anschauen 2/1.1; **watch television** fernsehen 6/4.1
water Wasser 5/13.1
watercress Kresse 8/7
way home Heimweg 7/2.1
wear tragen 6/1.1
weather Wetter 10/9.1
wedding Hochzeit 12/4.1
Wednesday Mittwoch 6/9.1
week Woche 3/10.1
weekend Wochenende 6/5.3
welcome to willkommen bei/zu 2; **you're welcome** gern geschehen, bitte 5/7.2
well gut 11/3; **well, ...** nun, ... 1/6
Welsh Waliser/in, walisisch 1/10.3
west Westen 5/13.3
what? was? 1/7; welche/r/s, was für (ein/e)? 5/4; **what time?** um wieviel Uhr? 6/5.2; **what do you do?** was machst du/machen Sie/macht ihr (von Beruf)? 1/7
when? wann? 6/5.3; **when** wenn 6/1.1; als 12/4.1
where? wo? 1/7.1; **where** *(Relativpronomen)* wo 4/3.3; **where ... from?** woher? 1/7.1
whether ob 8/3.1
which? welche/r/s? 3/8; **which** *(Relativpronomen)* der/die/das, welche/r/s 4/3.3
white weiß 5/4
who? wer? 1/11; wen? 7
whole ganz 5/13.1
why? warum? 2/1
wife *pl.* **wives** (Ehe-)Frau 1/8.1
will werden *(Zukunft)* 8.3/1
window Fenster 5/9.1
wine Wein 9/1.2
winner Gewinner/in 2/8.2
with mit 1/8.1
without ohne 7/1.1
woman *pl.* **women** Frau 4/6.3
wonderful wunderbar, wunderschön 4/7
wood Wald 12/8.1
word Wort 1/13
word map Wortnetz 5/9.3
work Arbeit 2/1.1; arbeiten 1/8.1
working week Arbeitswoche 8/7
world Welt 11/1.1
write schreiben 2/1.1
write down aufschreiben 5/8.2
write out ausschreiben 8/8.1
wrong falsch, inkorrekt 4/1.3

Y

yard AE Garten 5/13.1
year Jahr 4/1.2
yellow gelb 5/4
yes ja 1/1.2
yourself du/Sie (selbst) 6/8.4

UNIT 1: HOW ARE YOU?

1 A visit

1.1 Jane: Hello, Sarah. Come in. How are you?
Sarah: Fine thanks. How are you?
Jane: Just fine. Busy, but fine. Bob and Jim are in here. Come in.
Jane: Sarah, this is Bob. Bob, this is Sarah.
Sarah: Pleased to meet you.
Bob: Pleased to meet you.
Jane: And this is Jim.
Jim: Hello.
Sarah: Hello, Jim.
Jane: Now then, a cup of coffee?
Sarah: Yes, please.

7 What do you do?

7.2 – Are you from Germany?
– Yes, I am.
– Where's your home now?
– It's here in Berlin.
– Where are you from?
– I'm from Frankfurt.
– What do you do?
– I'm a secretary.

8 Personal interviews

8.1 a)
Sarah: What do you do, Bob?
Bob: I'm a teacher.
Sarah: Are you and your wife from here in Lancaster?
Bob: No, we aren't. We're from Wales.

b)
Sarah: What do you do, Jane?
Jane: I'm a secretary.
Sarah: Are you from here?
Jane: No, I'm not. I'm really from London, but my home's here now.
Sarah: Your name's MacGregor, isn't it?
Jane: Yes, it is.
Sarah: Are your parents Scottish?
Jane: Well, my father's from Scotland, but my mother's from England.

c)
Sarah: What about you, Jim? What do you do?
Jim: Well, I have two jobs. I'm a painter and a house-husband!
Sarah: A house-husband?
Jim: Yes, my wife, Betty, is a doctor. I stay at home with the children. I work at home too, in my studio.
Sarah: You're American, right?
Jim: Yes, I am from Chicago. But my wife's English. She's from Lancaster.

UNIT 2: WELCOME TO EUROLINGUA

1 Why English?

1.1 Monika: I want to learn English for pleasure. I like languages and I like school. I want to speak English and I want to understand English songs.

Jürgen: I need English for my work. I want to write English letters and I want to meet people from other countries.

Silke: I want to learn English for holidays. I have friends in Ireland and I want to go to Dublin on holiday.

UNIT 3: HOME

2 The plural

2.1 1 books 2 cats 3 chairs 4 lamps 5 photographs 6 telephones 7 bookcases 8 oranges 9 glasses 10 matches 11 shelves 12 children

6 Pronunciation

6.1 cat ten friend family have empty shelf apple twelve then can match

8 A study

a)
There are two chairs and an armchair. There's a desk next to the computer. On the sofa there's a cat. There's a lamp on the desk. There are two dictionaries. There isn't a rug. There's an English newspaper under the coffee-table.

b)
There's a rug in front of the television. There isn't a video. There's a cat on the rug and a cat under the coffee-table. On the shelf there are three photos and a German-English dictionary. There is a bookcase next to the desk. There's an English newspaper on the coffee-table.

c)
There's a bookcase behind the television. There are four books in the bookcase. An English-German dictionary is on the shelf. There are two chairs and a desk. The desk is next to the computer. There isn't a television. There are three photographs and four cats on the shelf.

UNIT 4: FAMILY

8 Pronunciation

8.1 I have a small cup and a large glass. My mother loves London, but my father likes the country. My brother is in the garden. You are number one. Is love the answer? It is summer.

8.2 She likes short conversations. We watch English television. Jim is a German teacher. The question is on page ten. The orange is on the chair. Jane's old furniture is in the garage.

UNIT 5: AT THE MARKET

1 The apples are sixty pence a pound

1.1 The lemons are 20 pence each.
The oranges are 25 pence each.
The potatoes are 28 pence a pound.
The onions are 30 pence a pound.
The cucumbers are 36 pence each.
The carrots are 40 pence a pound.
The beans are 45 pence a pound.
The tomatoes are 48 pence a pound.
The peas are 50 pence a pound.
The bananas are 56 pence a pound.
The apples are 60 pence a pound.
The pears are 65 pence a pound.
The peaches are 70 pence a pound.
The apricots are 72 pence a pound.
The plums are 78 pence a pound.
The melons are 80 pence each.
The strawberries are 88 pence a pound.
The blueberries are 90 pence a pound.
The raspberries are 96 pence a pound.
The pineapples are £1 each.
The mushrooms are £1.20 a pound.
The cherries are £1.30 a pound.

8 Numbers

8.3 Good morning shoppers! Here are today's special offers:

Golden Delicious apples	40p a pound
Small tin of tomatoes	only 17p
Frozen chicken	80p a pound
Free-range eggs	£1.50 a dozen
Cheddar cheese	£1.19 a pound
Oranges	only 18p each

Don't miss these great offers!

UNIT 6: ROUTINES AND HABITS

3 The present simple: verbs in the third person singular

3.1 1 he drinks 2 she comes 3 it finishes 4 he waits 5 she misses 6 she sleeps 7 he goes 8 she wears 9 she speaks 10 he watches 11 he uses 12 she loves 13 he likes 14 he listens 15 she writes 16 he has

UNIT 7: QUESTION TIME

1 An interview with a country musician

1.1 Sarah Ford: Who writes the songs in your group?
Rickie Williams: We write the songs together. First the other members write the music and then I write the lyrics.
Sarah: What instruments do you play?
Rickie: I play the guitar and the banjo. And I sing, of course.
Sarah: Who's your favourite musician?
Rickie: My favourite musicians are Elvis Presley and Beethoven.
Sarah: Who do you prefer?
Rickie: I think I prefer Elvis.
Sarah: What's the name of your new album?
Rickie: The name is "Tennessee Dreams".
Sarah: Which song on your new album do you like best?
Rickie: I like all the songs. But "Days without you" is my favourite.

1.2 Sarah: When does your new album come out?
Rickie: Our new album comes out next month.
Sarah: Where do you live?
Rickie: I live in Atlanta, but I want to move to Nashville, Tennessee soon.
Sarah: Why do you want to live in Nashville?
Rickie: Our record company is in Nashville and the other band members live there too.
Sarah: What does your wife do?
Rickie: My wife? She's our manager.
Sarah: How old are your children?
Rickie: Jonny is seven and Patsy eleven years old.
Sarah: How do they like your music?
Rickie: Oh, they like it very much. Sometimes they come to our concerts.

UNIT 8: FOOD AND DRINK

3 Are they typical?

3.1 a)

Sarah: What do you normally have for breakfast, John?
John: Well, I normally have either a bowl of porridge or a bowl of muesli, and sometimes some toast.
Sarah: And what do you drink with it?
John: A cup of tea.
Sarah: What's your main meal?
John: Well, it depends. During the week when I'm at work, it's usually supper. And at the weekend when I'm at home, it's lunch.
Sarah: Mm. What snacks do you eat between meals?
John: ...um ... I rarely eat snacks. I occasionally have a chocolate biscuit, if I can find one.

b)

Sarah: And you Sue? What do you normally have for breakfast?
Sue: I have either muesli with fruit juice or a piece of toast with marmalade or jam.
Sarah: Do you have tea for breakfast?
Sue: No, I always drink coffee. I never drink tea.
Sarah: And what's your main meal?
Sue: ... um... Supper, yes.
Sarah: And what snacks do you eat between meals?
Sue: I often eat fruit and ... in the evenings crisps.

c)

Sarah: What do you normally have for breakfast, Mary?
Mary: Oh, eggs, sometimes tomatoes on toast.
Sarah: And what do you drink with it?
Mary: Tea, lots of tea.
Sarah: What's your main meal?
Mary: Dinner, at about 6.30 to 7.
Sarah: What snacks do you eat between meals?
Mary: Um, chocolates. Too many.

UNIT 10: LIKES AND DISLIKES

2 What kind of films do they like?

2.2 a)

Sarah: What kind of films do you like, Jane?
Jane: I like interesting films. You can learn something from them.
Sarah: You mean documentary films.
Jane: Yes, that's right. I like documentary films.
Sarah: Do you like romance or war films?
Jane: No, I don't like them. They're not realistic.

b)
Sarah: What do you think of war films, Kevin?
Kevin: You mean films like the ones about Vietnam?
Sarah: Yes, those.
Kevin: I don't like them. They're too violent.
Sarah: What about romance films? Films like Love Story?
Kevin: Well, I don't mind them. Sometimes they're interesting and sometimes they're boring.
Sarah: Do you like documentaries?
Kevin: Oh no! They're always boring. I hate them. I like films with action.

6 Word order

6.1
1. Hello, Robert. This is Richard. I can't meet you for lunch tomorrow. I'll call you at your office in the morning. Bye.
2. Hi, it's Sally! Lorna, I'll call you back later. It's about the party at Mary's house on Saturday.
3. This is Ann Landers calling for Lorna. Please call me at home this evening. The number is 682 4556.
4. This is Fred Miller of Worldwide Travel. Mr King, can you pick up your travel documents from our office before 8 o'clock tonight? If not, please call us.

UNIT 11: SUGGESTIONS

1 Would you like to come with me?

1.1 Sandra: Hello there, Lorna.
Lorna: Hi Sandra. Nice to see you. How are you?
Sandra: Oh, I'm great! I have this wonderful new job at the Hotel International and I love it!
Lorna: Oh really? That's great. What do you do?
Sandra: I'm a switchboard operator. It's very interesting. I talk to so many people from all over the world and I can use my French and Spanish too … Well, how about you, Lorna? How are you these days?
Lorna: Oh, just fine, thanks. Listen … I have an idea. Hugh Grant's new film is on at the Odeon cinema tonight. I'd like to see it. Would you like to come with me?
Sandra: That sounds nice. Yes, I'd love to come.
Lorna: Let's have a drink first. We can meet at the pub next to the cinema.
Sandra: Yes, fine. What time?
Lorna: Is 7.30 alright? The film starts at 8.30.
Sandra: Okay. See you later. Bye, Lorna.
Lorna: Bye, Sandra.

UNIT 12: CHILDHOOD MEMORIES

6 Regular verbs

1 arrived 2 asked 3 danced 4 hated 5 lived 6 loved 7 opened 8 stayed 9 needed 10 started 11 wanted 12 married 13 tried 14 dropped

ANSWER KEY

UNIT 1

1.1 Nein, denn Jane macht Sarah Ford mit Jim und Bob bekannt.

1.2 Bild 1: c, b; Bild 2: d, a; Bild 3: e

4
a) Hello. – Hi. – How do you do? – Good morning – Good afternoon. Good afternoon – Good evening. Good evening.
b) Pleased to meet you. – Nice to meet you.
c) Fine, thanks. How are you? – Fine, thanks.
d) Goodbye. – Bye. – Good night. Good night.

5.1 This is a visit. Good evening. Come in. Pleased to meet you, Jean. Jim is busy.

5.2 This is nice. Hi, Jim. I'm fine in the morning. Good night. Bye.

6
Manuel: Hello, Björn. How are you?
Björn: Hello, Manuel. I'm fine, thanks. How are you? (And you?)
Manuel: Fine thanks (I'm fine too, thank you.) Laura, this is Björn. Björn, this is Laura.
Björn: Hello, Laura. Nice to meet you. (Pleased to meet you.)
Laura: Hello, Björn. Nice to meet you too. (Pleased to meet you too.)
Laura: Well, there's my taxi. Bye, Björn. Bye, Manuel.
Björn: Bye, Laura.
Manuel: Bye, Laura.

7.1 1c – 2d – 3b – 4a

8.1

name	job	from	home now
Bob	teacher	Wales	Lancaster
Jane	secretary	London	Lancaster
Jane's father	–	Scotland	–
Jane's mother	–	England	–
Jim	painter and house-husband	Chicago	Lancaster
Betty	doctor	Lancaster	Lancaster

8.3 2. No, she isn't. 3. Yes, it is. 4. No, they aren't. 5. No, she isn't. 6. No, they aren't. 7. Yes, he is. 8. No, she isn't.

10.1
Aussage: you're – you are – he/she/it's – he/she/it is – we/you/they're – we/you/they are
Verneinung: he/she/it isn't – he/she/it is not – we/you/they aren't – we/you/they are not
Frage: Where am I? Where are you? Where's he/she/it? / Where is he/she/it? Where are we/you/they?

10.2 1. I'm – wife's – She's 2. It's – It's 3. We're – They're 4. father's – He's – mother's 5. you're – you're 6. We're – That's – You're

10.3 is – am – is – is – are not – are – is – are not – are – is – is – are

13
Familienmitglieder: wife, husband, father, mother, parents
Berufe: secretary, teacher, painter, doctor
Länder: England – English; Germany – German; Scotland – Scottish; Wales – Welsh; United States of America – American; Switzerland – Swiss; Austria – Austrian; Ireland – Irish; (Great) Britain – British

UNIT 2

1.1 I want to learn English for pleasure / for holidays – I need English for my work – I want to speak English / write English letters / understand English songs – I have relatives or friends in an English-speaking country – I want to go to Great Britain or to America on holiday – I like languages – I like school.

2.1 1g – 2c – 3i – 4a – 5b – 6j – 7d – 8f – 9e – 10h

2.4 Lösungsbeispiele
Sport: Badminton, Basketball, Bodybuilding, Fitnessclub, Golf, Jogging, Mountainbike, Squash, Surfing, Swimmingpool, Tennis, Volleyball
Essen und Trinken: Bananasplit, Brunch, Cheeseburger, Chips, Cocktail, Dinner, Drink, Grapefruit, Hamburger, Happy Hour, Hotdog, Ketchup, Milkshake, Popcorn, Roastbeef, Snack, Steak, Toast
Unterhaltung (Musik, Film, Fernsehen, Printmedien): Action, Bestseller, CD, Clown, Comeback, Comic, Discman, Disco, Entertainer, Filmstar, Flop, Gameboy, Hifi, Hit, Interview, Jazz, Live(-Musik), LP, Punk, Reggae, Rock'n' Roll, Science Fiction, Single, Showbusiness, Star, Talkshow, Thriller, Video, Walkman, Western
Kommunikationstechnologie: CD-Rom, Computer, Disc, Hardware, Internet, Joystick, Laptop, Notebook, Printer, Scanner, Software
Flugverkehr/Raumfahrttechnik: Airport, Cockpit, Economy Class / Business Class / Tourist Class, Gate, Jet, Shuttle, starten, Terminal, Ticket
Berufswelt: Barkeeper, Deal, Handy, Manager, Meeting, Public Relations, Publicity, Service, Steward/ess, Stress
Mode und Einkaufen: Body(stocking), Duty-free-Shop, No-name-Produkt, Non-book(-Abteilung), Non-food (-Abteilung), Shop, Shopping, Shopping-Center

4.1 páradise – Paradís; éssence – Esséntz; quálity – Qualitắt; univérsity – Universitắt; wélcome – Willkómmen; generátion – Generatión; míneral – Minerál; nátural – natürlich

4.2 Scótland – Íreland – Áustria – Swítzerland Américan – évening – afternóon – hólidays – párents – fámily – húsband stúdent – teácher – pérsonal – rélatives – sécretary

6.3 secretary – chair – English – learn – write – pleasure

7 1. school 2. work 3. listen 4. write 5. read 6. want 7. pleasure 8. meet 9. speak 10. learn 11. holidays 12. people

8.1 a) 1. Contents Chart 2. Dictionary 3. Tapescript 4. Answer Key
b) 1. Seite 117 2. Seite 126 3. Seite 131 4. Seite 4, 5 und Seite 26
c) 1d – 2a – 3g – 4h – 5b – 6e – 7f – 8c

8.2 a) A. Learning to Learn B. Language in Use C. Grammar
b) 1. C 2. B 3. A 4. B 5. A 6. C
c) 1. Dear Hans – (With) love, / Lots of love, / All my love, Elsa (Stichwort im Index „Briefe")
2. 20°C (Stichwort „Fahrenheit/Celsius")
3. potato chips (Stichwort „Amerikanisches Englisch")
4. trousers (Stichwort „Amerikanisches Englisch / Kleider")

9 A (Lerntechniken): Techniken zum Vokabellernen für unterschiedliche Lernertypen
B (Sprachgebrauch in Alltagssituationen): das Haus oder die Wohnung beschreiben
C (Grammatik): der bestimmte und unbestimmte Artikel; Plural der Nomen
Der Text „British homes" und die englischen Wohnungsanzeigen lassen sich nicht zuordnen, denn sie enthalten landeskundliche Informationen.
Nicht eindeutig zuordnen lassen sich „Möbel- und Einrichtungsgegenstände benennen" (= Vokabular) und „angeben, was sich wo befindet (there is / there are; Ortspräpositionen)" (= Sprachgebrauch in Alltagssituationen, Grammatik und Wortschatz).

UNIT 3

1.1 1. an armchair 2. a key 3. a cat 4. an exercise book 5. a telephone 6. a pen 7. a lamp 8. a desk 9. a computer 10. an English-German dictionary 11. an umbrella 12. a book 13. a fireplace 14. a newspaper 15. a match 16. a cup and saucer 17. a coffee-table 18. a teapot 19. an orange 20. an apple 21. a sofa 22. a video 23. a television 24. a shelf 25. a photograph 26. stereo 27. a chair 28. a bookcase 29. a glass 30. a bottle 31. a plant

1.2 a/an = ein, eine; an steht vor Wörtern, die mit a, e, i, o, u anlauten

2.1 [z], [s]: 1, 2, 3, 4, 5, 6, 11
[ɪz]: 7, 8, 9, 10
other: 12

2.2 cats – chairs – lamps – photographs – telephones – bookcase – orange – glass – match – shelf – children

2.3 [z], [s]: books, cats, chairs, lamps, photographs, telephones, shelves
[ɪz]: bookcases, oranges, glasses, matches
Bei Wörtern mit den Endlauten [s], [ʒ] oder [ʃ] („Zischlaute“) wird die Pluralendung [ɪz] gesprochen.

2.4
1. Beim regelmäßigen Plural wird an das Wort ein -s angehängt, z.B. cats.
2. Wenn das Wort auf -s oder -ch endet, wird -es angehängt, z.B. glasses.
3. Wörter, die auf Konsonant +y enden, haben im Plural die Endung -ies, z.B. dictionary – dictionaries oder secretary – secretaries.
4. Einige Wörter haben eine unregelmäßige Pluralform, z.B. child – children, shelf – shelves.

4.1 3. <u>the</u> orange 5. <u>the</u> umbrella 7. <u>the</u> apple 9. <u>the</u> English dictionary 11. <u>the</u> American newspaper

4.2 the wird [ðɪ] ausgesprochen vor Wörtern, die mit einem Vokal anlauten.

5.1 under the table – in front of the sofa – behind the lamp – next to the bookcase – between the computer and the stereo

6.1 [æ]: cat, family, have, apple, can, match
[e]: ten, friend, empty, shelf, twelve, then

6.2 [eɪ]: <u>name</u>, <u>table</u>, <u>radio</u>, <u>Jane</u>, <u>Wales</u>, <u>stay</u>, <u>they</u>, <u>eight</u>

7.2
a) furniture: armchair, bookcase, chair, coffee-table, desk, shelf, sofa
things for daily use: book, bottle, computer, cup and saucer, English-German dictionary, exercise book, glass, key, lamp, match, newspaper, pen, photograph, stereo, teapot, telephone, television, umbrella, video
b) bedroom: bed, bedside table, chest of drawers, mirror, rug, wardrobe
kitchen: coffee maker, cooker, cupboard, dishwasher, freezer, microwave, refrigerator, sink, table, washing-machine
bathroom: bath-tub, sink, toilet, mirror, shower, washing-machine
c) Hören kann man z.B.: refrigerator, washing-machine, freezer, dishwasher, coffee maker, shower, toilet, radio, television, video, telephone, computer etc.
Riechen kann man z.B. plants, apples, oranges, fireplace, refrigerator, dishwasher, washing-machine, coffee maker, cat etc.

8 Description b)

10.1 balcony: balc – bathroom: bath – bedroom: bed – dining room: din rm – fitted: fit – flat: flt – fully-fitted kitchen: ff kit – furnished: furn – garage: gge – house: hse – kitchen: kit – large: lge – living room: liv rm – luxury: lux – near: nr – per week: pw – reception room: recep – separate: sep – shower: shwr – studio apartment: studio apt – unfurnished: unfurn

10.2 The best house for the Brown family is the house in KENSINGTON. The rent is £195 per week and there are 3 bedrooms.

10.3 Lösungsbeispiel
Berlin – SCHÖNEBERG near KaDeWe. Lge studio apt with sep ff kit & bath, balc, gge. 800 DM, 030 / 786 99 57

UNIT 4

1.1 Bild 1: Lynn, Robert; Bild 2: Maria

1.3 Lynn lives in <u>New York</u>. Every year she goes to <u>Canada</u> on holiday. Her <u>children</u> have a house there. Its garden is very nice. Lynn's husband is from <u>Austria</u>. His name is Robert. He is a <u>computer programmer</u> for British Airways. Lynn has a <u>son</u> in California. His name is Jack. His daughter's name is Sharon. She is <u>fifteen</u>. Jack works for an American <u>airline</u>. Its name is Microdisk. Lynn has a <u>brother</u> and a <u>sister</u>. Their names are Andrew and Anne. Anne speaks <u>French</u> and wants to go to university in Germany. Lynn and Robert's neighbours are German. They're from <u>Salzburg</u>, but they live in England now.

1.4 London – Scotland – parents – Canada – pilot – brother – five – computer firm – son – daughter – German – Berlin

2.1 linke Spalte: your husband – my brother – his name – our son
rechte Spalte: your daughter – ihr Name – ihr Name – ihr Garten

2.2 your – his – her – its – our – their

2.3 Den Genitiv mit -s verwendet man für Personen. Den Genitiv mit of verwendet man für Sachen.
Lynn's husband – Jack's girlfriend – his daughter's name – Lynn and Robert's neighbours – my parents' house – the name of the firm

3.2.

What's	the president's your teacher's her friend's your father's his parents'	name? telephone number? address?
What's	the name the telephone number the address	of the hotel? of the restaurant? of the computer firm?

3.3 1. His name is Robert. 2. His name is Jack. 3. His name is Andrew. 4. Her name is Anne. 5. Its name is Microdisk. 6. Her name is Sharon. 7. Her name is Maria. 8. Their names are Andrew and Anne. 9. Their names are Lynn and Robert. 10. Its name is British Airways.

3.4 My – Her – His – Their

5 linke Spalte: works – looks – wants – speaks – starts
rechte Spalte: lives – likes – goes – has – is

7 are – am – am – like – are – have – is – is – lives – comes – is – wants – have – has – likes – works – has – are – is – want

8.1 [ʌ]: cup, mother, love(s), London, but, country, brother, number, one, summer
[ɑː]: large, glass, father, garden, answer

8.2 [ʃ]: she, short, conversations, English
[tʃ]: watch, teacher, question, chair, furniture
[ʒ]: television, garage
[dʒ]: Jim, German, page, orange, Jane

Option 1

1.1 a bar, a milkshake, a hamburger, a taxi, an interview, a film star, an American film star, a T-shirt, a clown, a manager, an English manager, a mountain bike, a yoghurt, an inter-city, an English film, a ticket, a baseball, a university, an Austrian university, a party, a cocktail, a hobby, an old hobby

2 1. No, it isn't. 2. No, there isn't. 3. Yes, she is. / No, she isn't. 4. No, they aren't. 5. Yes, I am. / No, I'm not. 6. Yes, it is. 7. Yes, I am. / No, I'm not. 8. No, you aren't. 9. Yes, I am. / No, I'm not. 10. Yes, there is. / No, there isn't. 11. Yes, we are. 12. Yes, he is. 13. Yes, there are. / No, there aren't. 14. Yes, he is. / No, he isn't. 15. Yes, he/she is. / No, he/she isn't. 16. Yes, there are. 17. No, we aren't. 18. No, they aren't.

3.1
1. No, he isn't a pilot. He's a doctor.
2. No, there aren't three televisions in the picture. There are four plants.
3. No, I'm not the teacher. I'm a student.
4. No, this isn't Ireland. This is (Great) Britain.
5. No, the car isn't from England. It's from Germany.
6. No, they aren't in the United States. They are in Germany.
7. No, she isn't in the living room. She's in the kitchen.

3.2 Lösungsbeispiele
1. Are they in San Francisco? – No, they aren't in San Francisco. They are in London.
2. Is this a television? – No, this isn't a television. This is a radio.
3. Are there three chairs in the picture? – No, there aren't three chairs in the picture. There are a chair, a table and a shelf.
4. Is she a computer programmer? – No, she isn't a computer programmer. She is a painter.
5. Is his name John Miller? – No, his name isn't John Miller. His name is John Smith.

4.1 is/comes – Bristol – is – Her – is – David – 's – works – have – Their – are – likes – German – wants – Scotland

4.2 Lösungsbeispiele
1. His name is Mark Rogers. He is from Kansas in the United States, but his home is Toronto in Canada now. He is a teacher. He has one son. His name is Tommy. He is fifteen. Mark Rogers likes holidays and good restaurants. He wants to go to California for his next holiday.
2. Their names are Alistair and Beverley McDonald. They are from Scotland, but their home is in Switzerland now. Alistair is a manager in a Swiss computer firm and Beverley is a secretary. They have two children. Their names are Susan and Amanda. Susan is twenty and Amanda is twenty-four. Alistair and Beverley like Scotland. They go on holiday to Scotland every year.

5.1 Who is that? – What is his name? – How old is he? – Where is he?

6.1 its – your – his – their

6.2 1. It's 2. You're – your 3. His – He's 4. they're – their

7.1 Things: bottle and glass, chair and table, coffee and tea, cup and saucer, garden and house, pen and paper, radio and television
People: brother and sister, children and parents, daughter and son, friend and partner, husband and wife
Verbs: come and go, ask and answer, listen and speak, read and write
Time: morning and evening

7.2 to write a book / a song / a letter / a word – to understand a book / English / a language / a letter / a newspaper / a question / a song / your teacher / a word – to spell a word – to speak English / a language – to read a book / a letter / a newspaper / a word – to own a book / a flat / a house – to live in a flat / a house – to listen to a question / the radio / a song / your teacher / a word – to learn English / a language / a song / a word – to ask a question / your teacher

8.2
1. [æ]: can, balcony, address, that, match, have, has, lamp
   [eɪ]: tape, page, make, table
   [aː]: glass, garden, start, after, are
2. [e]: spell, twelve, French, then, well, every, hotel, bed, next
   [ɪ]: he, English, be, she, England
3. [ɪ]: film, six, picture, with, morning, children, fill, in, think, live, thing
   [aɪ]: like, write, pilot, night, child, dialogue, time, nine, right, five
4. [ɪ]: very, family, balcony, twenty, empty
   [aɪ]: my, goodbye, why

9 1. das Haus ganz rechts 2. der Wohnwagen oben 3. das moderne Wohnhaus unten

UNIT 5

1.1 Potatoes: 28p a pound – Cucumbers: 36p each – Beans: 45p a pound – Tomatoes: 48p a pound – Bananas: 56p a pound – Apricots: 72p a pound – Plums: 78p a pound – Strawberries: 88p a pound – Raspberries: 96p a pound – Cherries: £1.30 a pound

2.1 Peter kauft ein Pfund Äpfel und vier Orangen. Die Frau nennt ihn love.

4 red: tomatoes, strawberries, raspberries, plums, cherries, apples
yellow: bananas, lemons, pineapples, apples, pears
blue: blueberries, plums
green: pears, melons, beans, peas, cucumbers, apples
orange: peaches, apricots, carrots
brown: potatoes, mushrooms, onions
white: onions, mushrooms

5.1 1. Can I have – please 2. How much is – How much are 3. that's all.

8.2 thirty-two – forty-three – fifty-four – sixty-five – seventy-six – eighty-seven – ninety-eight – a/one hundred – one hundred and fifty – three hundred and seventy-five – five hundred – nine hundred and ninety-nine

8.3 apples: 40p – tomatoes: 17p – chicken: 80p – eggs: £1.50 – cheese: £1.19 – oranges: 18p

9.1 Für Dinge und Personen, die sich nahe beim Sprechenden befinden, verwendet man this.
Für Dinge und Personen, die etwas weiter weg sind, verwendet man that.

10.1 these – Those – those – This one – that one – These – those

10.2 One verwendet man nach this und that, wenn ein zuvor genanntes Nomen nicht wiederholt wird. This one verwendet man, wenn das zu bezeichnende Objekt nahe am Sprecher ist, that one, wenn es sich weiter entfernt befindet.
Pluralformen: this/this one – these; that/that one – those

10.3 1. These 2. Those 3. This – That 4. these – those 5. those 6. This 7. That 8. these 9. that

11.1 2. full 3. long 4. cheap 5. bad 6. small 7. small 8. interesting 9. new

12.2 álphabet – apártment – ápricot – bálcony – banána – cúcumber – cústomer éxercise – expénsive – fámily – fúrniture – ínteresting – néwsagent – phótograph – potáto – président – ráspberry – réstaurant – stráwberry – télephone – tomáto – umbrélla – végetable

13.1 holiday: vacation – flat: apartment – favourite: favorite – garden: yard – centre: center – cinema: movie theater – theatre: theater – shop: store – shop where you buy medicine, cosmetics, snacks and drinks: drugstore

13.2 1. False. They live in Boston. They are in York on holiday.
2. False. They have a holiday home in York.
3. True.
4. False. A lot of tourists come to York in the summer.
5. True.
6. True.

UNIT 6

1.2 We think numbers 1, 3, 5, 8 and 10 are tall stories.

2 is – finishes – is – drinks – goes – goes – comes – cooks – is – has – are – sleeps – wears – speaks

3.1 [s]: 1, 4, 6, 9, 13, 15
[z]: 2, 7, 8, 12, 14, 16
[ɪz]: 3, 5, 10, 11

3.2 [s]: he drinks, he waits, she sleeps, she speaks, he likes, she writes
[z]: she comes, he goes, she wears, she loves, he listens, he has
[ɪz]: it finishes, she misses, he watches, he uses

3.3 [s] spricht man nach stimmlosen Konsonanten (z.B. nach k, p, t).
[z] spricht man nach Vokalen und stimmhaften Konsonanten (z.B. nach m, n, r, v).
[ɪz] spricht man nach Zischlauten: s, ch, sh.

3.4 reads – listens – comes – writes – sleeps – drinks – stays – uses
watches – finishes – misses – matches
Ausnahmen: goes – has – is – can

5.1 School is OK for Diana.

5.2 eight – nine – five – nine – four
1. Yes, she does. 2. No, it doesn't. 3. No, she doesn't. 4. Yes, they do.

5.3 like – think – do – play – help – watch – do – go – go
1. No, he doesn't. He thinks it is boring. 2. He plays football. 3. Yes, he does. 4. He goes to bed at nine o'clock on Sundays. 5. No, he doesn't. He goes to bed at ten on Fridays. 6. Yes, they do.

5.4 1. That's true. 2. That's true. 3. That's false. She wears a uniform to school. 4. That's false. Her parents have a car. 5. That's true. 6. I don't know. 7. That's true. 8. I don't know.

6 Questions: I – you – we – they – he – she – it
Short answers:
linke Spalte: I – you – we – they – he – she – it
rechte Spalte: I – you – we – they – he – she – it
Negatives: I – you – we – they – he – she – it

7.1 No, Jean does not like Ben. Jean likes only things and people with an [iː] sound.

8.1 1c – 2g – 3b – 4a – 5e – 6i – 7h – 8d – 9j – 10f

9.1 Monday – Tuesday – Wednesday – Thursday – Friday – Monday – Tuesday, Wednesday – Thursday – Friday – Saturday – Sunday – Friday

9.2 Monday is blue, Tuesday and Wednesday are grey.

10.1 It's a quarter past twelve – It's five past one – It's ten to eleven – It's twenty-five past six – It's a quarter to five – It's twenty past nine – It's twenty-five to eight – It's ten past eight – It's twenty to six – It's ten past two – It's five to twelve – It's twelve o'clock – It's a quarter to four – It's half past eight.

10.3 half past three in the afternoon – eleven o'clock in the morning – five past one in the afternoon – a quarter past two at night – twenty-five to seven in the morning – a quarter to eleven in the evening/at night – five to six in the morning – a quarter to one in the afternoon – twenty-five past twelve at night

10.5 On – at – in – at – at – in – at – on – On – in – at – at

11
1. Children start school in Britain when they are five years old.
2. They are eleven years old when they go to secondary school.
3. They finish secondary school when they are sixteen.
4. There are comprehensive schools and grammar schools.
5. Public schools are not really public because they are very expensive.
6. Many British children wear a uniform.
7. The school day starts at nine o'clock.
8. It finishes at four o'clock.

Option 2

2.1 Lösungsbeispiele
to buy – bye; beer – dear; dear – here; bye – hi; cat – flat; a lot – hot; to eat – meat; meat – to meet; brother – mother; beach – peach; hi – pie; day – to play; night – right; to play – to say; pea – to see; pink – sink; long – song; son – sun; to say – to stay; small – tall; pear – there; to sing – thing; sink – to think; there – wear; no – window; song – wrong; all – small; to go – to know; how – now; cheese – these; bed – red; true – blue; old – cold; pen – men; white – right; here – year; sea – pea; drink – pink

3 1. chair 2. coffee maker 3. sink 4. cooker 5. freezer 6. table 7. cupboard 8. microwave. 9. refrigerator (You put food in it and the food stays cold.)

4 banana – orange – cheese – chicken – apple – potato
Don't put all your eggs in one basket.

5 one – two – four – five – six – seven – ten – twelve – sixty – eighty

6 1. wears 2. comes 3. plays 4. speaks 5. finishes 6. hates 7. sleeps 8. watches
Across: BREAKFAST

UNIT 7

1.1 1a – 2d – 3f – 4e – 5c – 6b

1.2 g. When does your new album come out? h. Where do you live? i. Why do you want to live in Nashville? j. What does your wife do? k. How old are your children? l. How do they like your music?

1.3 1. Who bedeutet auf deutsch wer und wen. Wenn who = wer, verwendet man in der Frage keine Umschreibung mit do/does.
2. What und which haben vor Nomen eine ähnliche Bedeutung: was für ein/e, welche/r/s. Bei der Frage nach einer begrenzten Zahl von Dingen oder Personen verwendet man which. Bei der Frage nach einer nicht begrenzten Zahl verwendet man what.

2.2 Lösungsbeispiele

Where ...	does Jim work?
	does Annie work?
	do they (all) have breakfast?
	is the children's school?
	does Annie buy food for supper?
What ...	does Jim like very much?
	does Annie do?
	does Annie do at 6.30?
	does Annie buy at the supermarket?
	do Jim and Annie watch on television?
Who ...	makes breakfast?
	goes to work at 7.30?
	drives the children to school?
	finishes work at three o'clock in the afternoon?
	goes to bed at 8 o' clock?
Who ...	does Annie wake at 7o'clock?
	does Annie drive to school?
	does Annie fetch from school at 3.15?
When ...	does Jim go to work?
	do Jim and Annie watch television?
Why ...	does Jim like his job?
	does Annie drive the children to school?
How ...	old are the children?
	long does Jim work?

4.1 Lösungsvorschläge
home: Where do you live? Do you have a garden or a balcony? Do you have a large or a small kitchen?
job: What do you do? Where do you work? Do you work in an office? Do you like your job? Why/Why not?
family: Do you have a large family? How old are your children? Do you have many brothers or sisters? Where do your parents live?
habits: Do you drive a car to work? What do you do at the weekend? Do you read a newspaper in the morning? When do you get up in the morning? When do you finish work?

5.1 1. b, c, e, f, g 2. a, d, j 3. l, m 4. n 5. h 6. i 7. k 8. o

5.2

English	German
1. watch	Armbanduhr
2. handbag	Handtasche
3. coat	Mantel
4. handkerchief	Taschentuch
5. during	während
6. tomorrow	morgen
7. scarf	Schal
8. purse	Portemonnaie
9. enough	genug
10. pocket calculator	Taschenrechner
11. money	Geld
12. address book	Adreßbuch
13. usually	normalerweise
14. lipstick	Lippenstift
15. notepad	Notizblock

6.1 a) 1. get up steht in einem ganzen Satz / typischen Kontext.
2. get up und go to bed bilden ein Gegensatzpaar.
3. Die vier Ausdrücke bilden eine chronologische Reihenfolge; sie stellen einen zeitlichen Ablauf dar.
4. get up ist Zentrum eines word map mit allgemeingültigen und persönlichen Assoziationen zum Thema „Aufstehen".

b) 1. news steht in einem ganzen Satz / typischen Kontext.
2. Die vier Wörter gehören zur gleichen Wortfamilie (Ableitungen von new, Zusammensetzungen mit news).
3. news steht in einem word map.

7

1. Tomatoes are red, carrots are orange, potatoes are brown.
2. Zum Beispiel: What do you do? Do you like your job? Where do you work?
3. Does she talk in her sleep? Does he drink beer? Does he eat meat? Does he play football?
4. eighty-three – ninety-nine – thirty-three – seventeen
5. I'm fine, thank you. / Fine, thanks. And you?
6. How do you do?
7. Pleased (Nice) to meet you.
8. Zum Beispiel: a sofa, an armchair, a coffee table, a television
9. fourteen – forty – eighteen – eighty
10. Zum Beispiel: tea, coffee, water, beer
11. twenty-five past eight in the morning – a quarter past four in the afternoon – half past six in the evening – eleven o'clock at night
12. Zum Beispiel: Where do you live? Do you live in a flat or in a house? Do you have a balcony/garden?
13. Zum Beispiel: apples, cherries, lemons, peaches
14. a
15. in
16. five to eight in the morning – twenty-five to nine in the evening – a quarter to four in the afternoon – twenty past one at night
17. I am from …
18. at/in
19. I don't talk in my sleep. I don't drink beer. I don't eat meat. I don't play football.
20. talk in your sleep – drink beer – eat meat – play football
21. What does "opposite" mean? What's the German word for "opposite"?
22. My home's … now. / I live in …
23. thirty-seven – forty-one – nineteen – ninety
24. How do you spell "breakfast"?
25. on
26. I get up at …
27. Zum Beispiel: cooker, refrigerator, coffee-maker, microwave
28. Zum Beispiel: Do you have many brothers and sisters? How old are your children? Do your parents live in …? Where does your sister live? How old is she?
29. Zum Beispiel: Do you have a hobby? Do you play football/rugby/tennis?
30. That's OK / all right. / Not at all. / You are welcome.
31. do
32. Zum Beispiel: purse, handkerchief, address book, keys
33. sister – husband – daughter
34. Zum Beispiel: Can I have a pound of apples, please?
35. My phone number is …
36. Zum Beispiel: How much are these strawberries?
38. Zum Beispiel: cucumbers, beans, peas
39. from – at – in
40. to
41. Zum Beispiel: I get up. I make breakfast. I go to work. I buy food at the supermarket.
42. No, thanks, that's all.
43. Thank you. How much is that?
44. their – at
45. Zum Beispiel: I don't smoke. I don't drink whisky. I don't drive a car. I don't wear glasses.
46. Zum Beispiel: I take a walk. I go to a restaurant. I watch television. I write letters. I read a good book.
47. drive
48. I go to bed at …
49. cheap – empty – new – short
50. Zum Beispiel: When do you get up in the morning? When do you go to bed at night? When do you come home from work? Do you read a newspaper every day? Do you smoke?

UNIT 8

1.1 1. bacon 2. tomato 3. fried egg 4. sausage 5. butter 6. toast 7. salt 8. pepper 9. sugar 10. jam 11. marmalade 12. milk 13. porridge 14. cereal 15. tea 16. honey 17. orange juice 18. bread 19. roll 20. coffee

2.2 1. False. Most people in Britain never have a traditional English breakfast. 2. False. Their main meal is supper at half past five or six o'clock. 3. True. 4. True. 5. True. 6. True. 7. False. Most people drink six or more cups of tea or coffee a day.

3.1

	breakfast	main meal	snacks
John	porridge or muesli, toast, tea	supper during the week, lunch at the weekend	chocolate biscuit
Sue	muesli and fruit juice or toast with marmalade or jam, coffee	supper	fruit, crisps in the evenings
Mary	eggs, tomatoes on toast, tea	dinner (at about 6.30 to 7)	chocolates

3.2 John is typical because he has cereal, toast and tea for beakfast and his main meal is supper. He is not typical because he rarely eats snacks (66 % of British people eat four or more snacks a day).
Sue is typical because she eats a continental-type breakfast of cereal and toast, her main meal is supper and she often eats snacks. She is not typical because she drinks coffee in the morning.
Mary is typical because she drinks tea for breakfast, has her main meal in the evening and eats a lot of snacks between meals. She is not typical because she has eggs and tomatoes on toast for breakfast.

4.1 always – usually/normally – often – sometimes – occasionally/rarely – never

4.3 *Adverbs of frequency* stehen meist <u>vor</u> dem Verb. Ausnahme: das Verb to be.

6.1 What do you normally have for breakfast?
Most people in Britain never have a traditional English breakfast.

8.1 go – how – home – house – phone – town

8.2 <u>A</u> lot <u>o</u>f wom<u>e</u>n smoke cig<u>a</u>rettes.
My broth<u>e</u>r <u>a</u>nd sist<u>e</u>r sleep fr<u>o</u>m ten t<u>o</u> elev<u>e</u>n in th<u>e</u> morning.

8.3 Zum Beispiel: drink, pink, sink, think, long, morning, sing, thing

9 1d – 2e – 3f – 4h – 5a – 6b – 7g – 8c

10.1 The singer doesn't say why there is no milk today, but there are different possibilities (Möglichkeiten):
1. His love has gone away and there is nobody to order (bestellen) the milk …
2. His love has gone away with the milkman …
3. Do <u>you</u> have a better idea (eine bessere Idee)?

UNIT 9

1.2 half a pound of butter – 10 slices of cheese – a dozen eggs – one or two packets of tea – a carton of milk – 7 bottles of wine

1.3 1. a bottle of wine 2. a loaf of bread 3. a carton of milk 4. a tin of anchovies 5. a packet of crisps 6. a box of chocolates 7. three slices of ham 8. a jar of (orange) marmalade 9. a glass of champagne

2.1 How many (dt.: wie viele?) verwendet man vor zählbaren Begriffen (Mehrzahlwörter).
How much (dt.: wieviel?) verwendet man vor nicht-zählbaren Begriffen (Einzahlwörter).

2.2 2. How much jam do we need? – Can you get one jar of (strawberry) jam, please?
3. How much champagne do we need? – We need one bottle of champagne.
4. How many boxes of chocolates do we need? – Can you get one box of chocolates, please?
5. How much milk do we need? – We need two cartons of milk.
6. How many packets of crisps do we need? – We need three packets of crisps.

7. How much bread do we need? – Can you get one loaf of bread.
8. How many eggs do we need? – We need a dozen eggs.
9. How much cheese do we need? – Can you get six slices of cheese?
10. How much tea do we need? – We need two packets of tea.
11. How many tomatoes do we need? – Can you get one pound of tomatoes?
12. How much cream do we need? – We need one carton of cream.
13. How many mushrooms do we need? – Can you get a quarter of mushrooms, please?
14. How much butter do we need? – We need half a pound of butter.

3.1 In Fragen und verneinten Sätzen verwendet man much oder many. In bejahten Sätzen verwendet man a lot of.

UNIT 10

2.2

	documentaries	romance films	war films
Jane	likes them; they are interesting	doesn't like them; they are not realistic	doesn't like them; they are not realistic
Kevin	hates them; they are boring	doesn't mind them; sometimes they are boring, sometimes interesting	doesn't like them; they are too violent

2.3 … She says she doesn't like romance films or war films because they are not realistic. Kevin says he hates documentaries because they are boring. He says he doesn't mind romance films. He thinks sometimes they are interesting and sometimes they are boring. He says he doesn't like war films because they are too violent.

5.1 Dialogue b)

5.2 Hello. 276 8765. – Hello. Could I speak to Sandra, please? – I'll get her for you. – This is (+ name). – Goodbye.

6.1
1. … at home this evening. – I'll call you at your office in the morning.
2. … at Mary's office on Friday. – It's about the party at Mary's house on Saturday.
3. … at my sister's house this afternoon. – Please call me at home this evening.
4. … after 8 o'clock tonight. – Mr King, can you pick up your travel documents from our office before 8 o'clock tonight?

6.2 Englisch: Ort vor Zeit Deutsch: Zeit vor Ort

6.3
1. Call me at the office before six o'clock.
2. It's about the party at Mike's house at the weekend.
3. I can't meet you at the market on Saturday.
4. Please pick up your tickets from our office this afternoon.

7.1 Bild 1: I love you. Do you love me too?
Bild 2: He loves her and she loves him.
Bild 3: Do you like them too?
Bild 4: The cat likes us. We like it too.

7.2 me – you – him – her – it – us – them

7.3 1. you – you 2. it 3. you 4. us 5. it 6. you 7. it – it 8. us – them 9. her – her – her 10. me – him

8.1 What a horrible opera. The doctor wants to take a walk. I want to go to the office tomorrow.

8.2 All lawyers talk. Call your daughter in Austria.

8.3 [uː]: two, spoons, beautiful, blue, do, you, fruit, newspaper, afternoon
[ʊ]: good, book, football, look, woman

8.4 boyfriend – toilet

9.1 1c – 2b – 3a – 4d a. France b. Germany c. the United States d. Austria

UNIT 11

1.1 1. Sandra works at the Hotel International. 2. She is a switchboard operator. 3. She loves it. She thinks it's very interesting. 4. She would like to go to the cinema to see Hugh Grant's new film. 5. They will meet at the pub next to the cinema at half past seven.

2.1
1. Hello there, Lorna.
2. Hi Sandra. Nice to see you. – How are you?
3. Oh, I'm great!
4. I have this wonderful new job. – I love it.
5. Oh really? That's great.
6. Well, how about you Lorna? How are you these days?
7. Oh, just fine, thanks.
8. Listen… I have an idea. – Hugh Grant's new film is on at the Odeon cinema tonight. I'd like to see it. Would you like to come with me?
9. That sounds nice. Yes, I'd love to come.
10. Let's have a drink first. We can meet at the pub next to the cinema.
11. Yes, fine. What time.
12. Is 7.30 all right? – The film starts at 8.30.
13. Okay. See you later. Bye, Lorna.

3 Parts **b)** and **d)** are new.

4.1
1. I'm not too well, I'm afraid.
2. I'm sorry to hear that. – That's too bad.
3. Yes, that's a good idea.
4. I'm sorry, I can't. I work evenings this week. But I could call you next week. We could go for a drink.
5. Thank you. Same to you.

5.1 Vorschläge
She can try to meet some of the other people at work. – She could talk to her boss. Perhaps she can do some other work in the hotel. – Why doesn't she find another job?

7.1 1. ~~dear~~ , first 2. ~~first~~, dear 3. ~~during~~ , wear 4. ~~four~~, during 5. ~~wear~~, four

7.2 1. The woman with the purple purse works on Thursday. 2. We're here, dear. 3. There are no pears on the chairs. 4. You're a tourist. 5. Where is your dog in the morning?

Option 4

4.1 1. cucumber ist kein Möbelstück. 2. small ist keine Farbe 3. interesting ist kein Verb.

UNIT 12

1.1 **a)** 1. Yes, they were. 2. No, she wasn't. 3. No, there wasn't. 4. No, there weren't. 5. No, he wasn't.
b) 1. Jack was three and his brother was four. 2. Their parents weren't at home. 3. It was at night. 4. It was black with yellow eyes. 5. The children were afraid.

1.2 Lösungsbeispiele
How old was Mrs Benson? Was the classroom small? Were there many other pupils? Was the blackboard green? What was the teacher's name? Was she English?

2.1 Positive statements: was – were – was – were
Negatives: wasn't – weren't
Questions: Was – were – Were

2.2 was – were – was – wasn't – was – were – weren't – was – wasn't – were

4.1 1b – 2e – 3a – 4c – 5d

5.1 lived – to live; had – to have; was – to be; took – to take; gave – to give; hated – to hate; tried – to try; could – can; were – to be; needed – to need; wanted – to want; started – to start; came – to come; said – to say; brought – to bring; sold – to sell; got – to get; saw – to see; fell – to fall; asked – to ask; did – to do; married – to marry; became – to become; made – to make; told – to tell; arrived – to arrive; found – to find; ate – to eat; opened – to open; ran – to run; stayed – to stay; thought – to think; slept – to sleep; woke up – to wake up; loved – to love; felt – to feel; went – to go; met – to meet; danced – to dance; dropped – to drop; sent – to send; knew – to know

5.2 Regular verbs: arrived – asked – danced – lived – loved – opened – stayed – hated – needed – started – wanted – married – tried – dropped
Irregular verbs: was – became – brought – came – did – ate – fell – felt – found – got – gave – went – had – knew – made – met – ran – said – saw – sold – sent – slept – took – told – thought – woke up – could

5.3
1. Die *past-simple*-Form der regelmäßigen Verben bildet man durch Anhängen von -ed.
2. Bei der Schreibung der regelmäßigen *past-simple*-Formen muß man folgendes beachten: Endet ein Verb
   - auf -e (z.B. like), wird nur ein -d angehängt (liked).
   - auf Konsonant + y (z.B. try), dann wird aus -y -i- (tried).
   - auf einen Konsonanten nach einem kurzen, betonten Vokal (z.B. stop), dann wird der Konsonant verdoppelt (stopped).
3. Die einzige Ausnahme ist das Verb to be.

6 [t]: 2, 3, 14
[d]: 1, 5, 6, 7, 8, 12, 13
[ɪd]: 4, 9, 10, 11
Nach den Endbuchstaben -t und -d spricht man die Endung -ed [ɪd] aus.

7
a) Monday – Tuesday – Wednesday – Thursday – Friday – Saturday – Sunday
b) Amanda ate an apple from Alabama.
Bill became a butler in Birmingham.
Bob brought Brenda a banana from Boston.
Kevin came with a cook from Kansas.
Diana did the dishes in Denver.
Fiona fell asleep in Florida.
Fred found four fried eggs in the freezer.
Gary gave his girlfriend a grey cat.
Greg got a great job in Greenville.
Harry had a holiday home in Florida.
Nina knew nothing about New York.
Mary made a milkshake in Miami.
Sally said that she was the sultan's secretary.
Susan saw some snow in Seattle.
Tina told Ted the true story about Tom.
Wendy went to work in Washington.
Walter woke up his wonderful wife in Wisconsin.

8 In the traditional fairy tale the wolf eats Little Red Riding Hood. In the fable by James Thurber, Little Red Riding Hood kills the wolf.

Option 5

2 Found – Opened – Read – Made – Sold – Offered – Felt – Took – Had – Ended – Paid – Ate – Said – Thought – Saw – Invited – Met – Played – Let – Explained

3 No, I didn't (did not) …

4 Lösungsbeispiele
Questions: Did Peter give you the letter yesterday? Did you go to New York? Did they send you a letter? Did Peter buy a television? What did you watch on television? When did the children get up? Where did Peter eat yesterday?
Negative sentences: Peter didn't give the children the newspaper. They didn't eat yesterday. Peter didn't buy a newspaper. The children didn't watch television. You didn't send Peter a letter. They didn't go to New York.

5 1b – 2c – 3a – 4d – 5e

ACKNOWLEDGEMENTS

For permission to reproduce photographs:

Bavaria: © Assmann, S. 107; © FPG, S. 16 (oben rechts), S. 67 – © Britische Zentrale für Fremdenverkehr, S. 60 (unten), S. 90 (unten rechts) – © 1995 EPS/Distr. Bulls, S. 18, S. 83 – © J. Allan Cash Ltd., S. 61 (rechts) – © Cornelsen, S. 32, S. 40 (links Mitte), S. 73 (unten), S. 85 (unten); Chipps, S. 17 (unten), S. 47 (oben), S. 80, S. 82, S. 87, S. 88, S. 92, S. 93, S. 94; Klaphake, S. 10, S. 13, S. 19, S. 30, S. 33, S. 34, S. 35, S. 40 (unten), S. 45, S. 46, S. 47 (unten), S. 50, S. 56, S. 57, S. 72, S. 75, S. 79, S. 85 (oben); Kleber, S. 73 (oben); Krauke, S. 16 (oben links, unten links, oben Mitte), S. 40 (oben), S. 73 (Mitte); Lücking, S. 81, S. 83 – © dpa, S. 84 (2. von rechts oben, links oben, 2. von links oben, 3. von links oben, 2. von rechts unten); dpa: © Dabrowski, S. 84 (3. von rechts oben); © European Press, S. 84 (links unten); © PA, S. 84 (rechts unten); © Persch, S. 84 (Mitte links); © Selector Press, S. 84 (Mitte rechts) – Focus: © Benn, S. 43 (unten rechts); © Blaustein, S. 43 (2. von links oben); © Burri/Magnum, S. 43 (oben links); © Platt/Onyx, S. 59; © Ravid/Onyx, S. 43 (unten Mitte); © Stock/Magnum, S. 52 (Mitte) – © Hoppe, S. 84 (2. von links unten) – Marco Polo: © Benejam, S. 43 (oben rechts); © Bouillot, S. 16 (unten rechts u. unten Mitte), S. 17 (oben), S. 36, S. 40 (rechts Mitte) – © Mirror Syndication International, S. 60 (oben), S. 61 (links), S. 77, S. 84 (rechts oben), S. 90 (links), S. 98, S. 99; Mirror Syndication International: © Hunter, S. 90 (oben rechts) – © The Ritz, S. 78 – © 1990 The Spectator, S. 74 – Transglobe Agency: © Ehlers, S. 52 (links); © Granitsas, S. 52 (rechts); © Halask, S. 43 (unten links) – © 1995 United Features Syndicate, Peanuts, S. 55, S. 109, S. 110.

For permission to reproduce copyright-material:

© David Higham Associates Ltd., Eleanor Farjeon, aus: “Silver Sand and Snow”, S. 63 – © Diesterweg, Margaret Clark, aus: “Time for a Poem”, S. 62 – © Fictions Songs Ltd., The Cure: “Friday I'm in love”, S. 59 – © Frederick A. Stokes Company, Annette Wynne, aus: “For Days and Days: A Year – Round Treasury of Verse for Children”, S. 62 – © Hournew Music Ltd., Graham Gouldman: “No milk today”, S. 77 – © Little, Brown & Co, Ogden Nash, aus: ”Custard and Company”, S. 62 – © Music Sales Ltd., Wanda Jackson: “Let's have a party”, S. 80; The Beatles: “Yesterday”, S. 108 – © Spike Milligan Productions Ltd., Spike Milligan, aus: “Silly Verse for Kids”, S. 62.

Nicht alle Copyrightinhaber konnten ermittelt werden; deren Urheberrechte werden hiermit vorsorglich und ausdrücklich anerkannt.